"They didn't discuss evidence at all, I wonder what that says about their system ... we spoke about it most of the time, I wonder what that says about ours."

English social worker, 1993

"All this talk of proof and evidence, the child is suffering, can't they see that?"

French social worker, 1993

To the children and families in Beauvais and London,
and their social workers.

Positive Child Protection: a View From Abroad

Andrew Cooper, Rachael Hetherington, Karen Baistow, John Pitts & Angela Spriggs

9

Russell House Publishing Ltd

First published in 1995 by

Russell House Publishing Limited
38 Silver Street
Lyme Regis
Dorset
DT7 3HS

British Library Cataloguing-in-Publication Data:
A catalogue record for this book is available from the British Library.

ISBN: 1-898924-35-X

Typeset by: EMS Phototypesetting, Berwick upon Tweed

Printed by: Hobbs The Printers, Southampton

Contents

Introduction

This book is concerned with the crisis in the child protection system of England and Wales and how it might be overcome. The implementation of the Children Act [1989] notwithstanding, child protection social work in England and Wales is still characterised by high professional anxiety, political ambiguity and a feeling of 'stuckness'. This is a product of the confusing and contradictory relationship which has come to exist between the law, the citizen, social work and the state in England. It is underpinned by the profound ambivalence of government to social intervention in families. Child protection social work in England has been bureaucratised, legalised and systematised. Meanwhile, social workers have been pilloried in the press and castigated by government. Yet, as far as we can tell, vulnerable children are no safer and the log-jam of unallocated child protection cases is undiminished.

But what can be learned about these problems by comparing the English child protection system with that of another country, especially one as different as France?

In our experience an initial fascination with the discovery that thirty miles from Folkestone they do things very differently was quickly supplemented by an enduring process of critical reflection on how we ourselves do things. The encounter with difference was comparable to looking in a mirror and being continually surprised not to see oneself, saying "Well, I don't look like that, so what do I look like, and how do I appear to them?" There is an obvious temptation to idealise another country's professional system and practices, particularly as English child protection work has been so beleaguered for what seems like the best part of a decade. In fact, to those who participated in this project it did seem that French practice was informed by a deep-rooted optimism all too rare in the experience of English practitioners, and the sources of both these collective states of mind are discussed in the following pages. However, in analysing the extraordinarily rich and diverse range of experiences reported by English practitioners during the research, our aim has not been to promote envy or self-flagellation, but to use comparison to help practitioners and managers see new possibilities, different ways of looking at familiar dilemmas, in short, to stimulate fresh and creative thought about both the broad sweep and the day to day task of child protection work in England.

The will towards partnership

The 1989 Children Act was implemented during the course of the research which informs this book. The principle of partnership, eagerly siezed on by the social work profession but much harder to render meaningful, is one among many themes about which we believe the French experience has much to teach us.

We found that French social workers, judges and most importantly parents and children involved in child protection cases, typically interact with one another against an unspoken background assumption of the right of every individual to belong to society. This contrasts with the increasing emphasis in English social work, and perhaps in British life, on disaggregated individual rights. In child protection work this trend is, we believe, in tension with the will towards partnership, and points to a central difficulty in realising the aspirations of the Children Act. But it is out of the belief that it is a difficulty, rather than an impossibility, that this book is written.

The presumption of non-intervention

Those principles informing the 1989 Children Act such as the 'presumption of non-intervention', which aim to support and develop intervention in the 'administrative' sphere of child protection, (as it is known in France), are held by many to embody its true spirit. As Parton (1991) has shown, the impetus of policy review in the 1980s towards the creation of a more flexible relationship between social work and the judiciary, and towards a properly preventative approach in child protection, came into severe tension with a trend towards increased legalism and interventionism in the wake of the succession of child abuse public enquiries in the second half of that decade. The contest for the heart of child protection work in England and Wales continues now. As the most recent Dartington Social Research Unit study (Bullock et al. 1993) shows, the majority of children who enter the public care system return to their families, or to some part of their family, when they leave care, and "The majority of these reunions occur in spite of the reasons for entering care or the length of time away." (1993 p.229) This finding points very clearly to the need not just to strengthen the means by which children may be prevented from entering the care system, but to recognise that child care work is a *process* rather than a set of discrete events surrounding children's entries to and exits from systems.

In France the 'administrative sphere' in child protection is better resourced and better organised than in England, and has at its hub the figure of the *Inspecteur* who carries organisational and moral authority with respect to child protection matters. As with the children's judge, this authority appears to derive from a broad social consensus which includes families who come to the attention of child protection services. This consensus reflects broad cultural and social assumptions about the place of the family in French society, and the relationship of the state to the family, which cannot be simply transposed to England. Nevertheless, if we are to realise the aspirations of the Children Act, it is to the equivalent part of our own system that we must direct attention, resources, and the attempt to legitimate our own consensus about the treatment of children, the responsibilities of parents, and location of non-judicial authority in these matters.

Positive child protection

In Section One we first give a picture of the experience of doing child protection social work in France, and what the quality of relationships might be like for workers and families, contrasting these with the experiences of people in comparable situations in England. Through this discussion we draw out some of the main similarities and differences between the two systems and point to the way in which day to day practices and global characteristics of the systems are always linked. We then describe the French system in more detail, with particular attention to the kinds of resources available and the roles of the main professional actors.

In Section Two we look more closely at the different spheres and levels of child protection work in France, concentrating on the typical experiences of children, families and social workers involved in both the administrative and judicial spheres. We start to examine different basic assumptions about what 'protecting children' means, and the consequences of the differing principles and methods informing social work practice in the two countries. These lead to different typical outcomes in the two countries for children and parents with similar initial difficulties. Rehabilitation to the family, the use of fostering and residential care, and adoption practices are all compared and contrasted, with continuing attention to the possibilities for English policy and practice.

In Section Three we concentrate attention on the contrasting professional cultures in which practitioners operate in France and England, and how these relate to wider aspects of political and social life. Different traditions of the state, social valuations of the family and basic assumptions about means and ends for political change all influence practice directly, and in each case reveal the inherent possibilities for practice in 'thinking it differently'. Protecting social workers is the related theme of the second part of this section, and we examine the differing responses of the media and of the courts to the social work role in child protection, and how these influence the quality and degree of professional anxiety experienced by workers in the two countries.

Finally, we draw together the strands of discussion and analysis in order to lay down a challenge for debate and change. The 1989 Children Act is a beginning, but no more than that, and if its spirit is to be made flesh, then a considerable effort of professional and political will is required. Practitioners, managers, policy makers, politicians, researchers, need to recover the confidence to mobilise in pursuit of a vision. To join Europe is not to be subsumed within one or other alien tradition or culture, but to exert influence and be open to influence. Our French colleagues are already absorbed in the process of adapting, innovating and creating as a result of their engagement in this project. Now it is our turn.

Throughout the text, the names of the social workers and their clients have been changed. Because the participating social workers were comparing the French child protection system with their experience of the system in England and Wales, not those of Scotland and Northern Ireland, we have referred throughout to 'English' rather than 'British' policy and practice. We hope that our Welsh friends and colleagues will not be offended by the fact that we use this rather than the correct but more cumbersome 'English and Welsh'.

About the Authors

Andrew Cooper is Principal Lecturer in Social Work at Brunel University College. He previously worked as a neighbourhood social worker and a generic fieldworker in inner London and as a residential child care worker in East London. He has a degree and an M.Phil in philosophy from Warwick University and trained as a social worker at the Polytechnic of the South Bank. His research interests include the place of psychoanalytic ideas and practices in modern welfare, and comparative European social work. His recent publications include 'In Care or en Famille – child protection, the family and the state in France and England', and 'The politics of *exclusion*', both in *Social Work in Europe*, and a study of the novels of John le Carré.

Rachael Hetherington is currently Senior Lecturer in Social Work at Brunel University College, having previously worked as a Psychiatric Social Worker and a Guardian ad Litem. She has an MA [Oxon], and a Diploma in Social Administration and a Diploma in Mental Health from the LSE. Her research interests include a comparative study of European child protection systems and the experiences of families involved in them in France and England. She is a member of the editorial board of *Social Work in Europe*. Her recent publications include 'Transmanche Partnerships' in *Adoption and Fostering*.

Karen Baistow is a Senior Lecturer in Psychology in the Departments of Social Work and Health and Paramedical Studies at Brunel University College. She has taught children with learning difficulties. She has a Masters degree in medical anthropology and her research interests include trans-national comparisons of the conceptual bases of professional practice in health and welfare and, in particular, the career of the notion of 'empowerment' in the fields of health and social welfare in Britain in the recent period.

John Pitts is Professor of Applied Social Science and Joint Head of the Department of Social Work at Brunel University College. He has worked as a printer, swimming pool maintenance operative, ceiling erector, cab driver, marketing executive, school teacher, youth worker, Intermediate Treatment development officer and group worker in a psychiatric Borstal. He holds degrees in criminology and has written and researched extensively in the fields of juvenile crime, justice and victimisation. His recent publications include: *The Politics of Juvenile Crime* [1988],

Working With Young Offenders [1990], *Developing Services For Young People in Crisis* [1991], *The Probation Handbook* [1992], *Probation Practice* [1995] and *Safer Schools, Safer Students* [1995].

Angela Spriggs is a researcher in the Department of Social Work at Brunel University College, Twickenham. She has a wide range of voluntary work experience including work with the National Trust, in a special needs boarding school, with the Probation Service, on an NCH Young Offenders' project and as an Adult Basic Education tutor. She has also worked in hotels and factories in Britain and Switzerland. She has a Masters degree in psychology from Dundee University and is currently involved in a comparative study of European child protection systems and the experiences of families involved in them in France and England.

Acknowledgements

The French end of the research upon which this book is based was undertaken by Alain Grevot and Véronique Freund of Association Jeunesse Culture Loisirs Technique (JCLT), Beauvais, l'Oise, and Jacques Bourquin, Nicole Brenot and Jean-Marie Camors of the Centre National de Formation et d'Etudes de la Protection Judiciare de la Jeunesse, Vaucresson, Paris.

The English research team comprised the authors and Brynna Kroll who, like Philip Smith the project administrator, worked long and hard with us to make sense of what we were learning.

Unfortunately, research protocols mean that we cannot name the social workers who participated in the project in France and England. They gave a great deal of time and unstinting commitment to the research and contributed enormously to the struggle to make sense of the differences we were encountering. They have been active participants, helping us to conceptualise the shared experience and suggesting new directions and refining hypotheses as the research unfolded. We are also indebted to the agencies in which research participants worked, who released them without demur.

Many other people have helped us in this work but, unfortunately, they cannot all be thanked here. Professor Michael King has offered advice and support from the inception of the project and we have appreciated the encouragement he has given us. We have also been encouraged by the active interest shown by Rupert Hughes at the DoH and Wendy Rose of the Social Services Inspectorate. At Brunel University College, David Whitehouse, Professor Margaret Yelloly and many other colleagues have taken an interest in our work and contributed to it in the staff seminars in which we have attempted to clarify our thoughts.

In Britain, the research upon which this book is based was funded by the Economic and Social Research Council, the European Commission (Directorate General 6), The British Council, The Florence Hallam Trust and the West London Institute Small Research Fund. In France funding was received from the Conseil General de l'Oise, Fondation de France, Uniformation, Ministére des Affaires Sociales, the European Commission (Directorate General 6), Caisse Nationale d'Allocations Familiales, Fondation pour l'Enfance and Association JCLT.

The Bar de la Gare, Beauvais, hosted a number of very boistrous international 'bébé football' matches during the research. The fact that the English team emerged victorious cannot have been easy to bear but the staff dealt with it with good grace, for which, many thanks.

Andrew Cooper
Rachael Hetherington
Karen Baistow
John Pitts
Angela Spriggs

Section One
La Différence

Chapter 1:
'Another Country'

A personalised practice

In the front room of a house just outside the town of Compiègne in northern France a meeting is taking place to discuss whether the mother and father of a child who has been the subject of a court order requiring social work intervention are willing to continue the work on a voluntary basis. The court order was a two year judicial AEMO, a kind of community supervision order and one of the commonest forms of statutory intervention in French child care work. Orders like this are made by the Children's Judge, the central legal figure in the child protection system, who remains involved with the family and is ultimately responsible for the case as long as the AEMO remains in force. Anne-Marie is the family's *éducatrice*, a specialist child care social worker. Jacques, who is manager of the small voluntary organisation for which she works, is also present. Eileen, an English social worker from a London local authority child care team has been invited to observe the meeting with the parents' consent. The atmosphere is relaxed, but business-like and quite formal. The parents address the two professionals as 'Madame' and 'Monsieur', which they reciprocate in their turn. A week later Eileen discusses her impressions of the meeting:

> "Anne-Marie felt that the father was agreeable to the work continuing but that the mother wasn't sure, so it was about getting her agreement. It was quite a successful meeting and they got the agreement that they could work for another year with the family. I think it was the mother who was unsure. There was no pressure at all, but the husband spoke, very articulately. It was unusual because often it's the fathers who are unwilling in these situations. I mean there was no explosion going on here or anything, it was all quite formal."
> "The family seemed to like their opportunity to meet the

2

judge, to go there and say their piece, whereas in England, at case conferences they don't really feel they're listened to. In my borough parents do attend the whole of conferences, which they don't in all places I think, but you still don't know how much they feel they can actually say in front of all those people. I think *we* feel intimidated in case conferences, so how do parents feel, I don't know? Whereas in France I feel parents welcome the idea of going to see the Judge; these people had obviously listened carefully to what the Judge had said, and the father particularly had felt listened to, had a chance to say his bit. Whereas in England, parents may say quite a lot when you visit them in their homes, but they feel tongue-tied in the conference, afraid to speak unless they incriminate themselves."

"I felt it had been very positive what the family had gained from the order. Yes, the mother was anxious, there was the fear that the children would be put in a placement, so Anne-Marie explained that this wasn't so, they were offering *help*... that the children might be cared for by foster parents during the day at times but that the contract was to continue in a voluntary way, and the father was quite keen and seemed happy to explain to the mother."

For Eileen, part of the fascination of this meeting was to encounter parents with a positive attitude to their experience of social work intervention in the context of a court order. Not only has the Children's Judge left a benign impression, particularly on the father, but both parents feel able to continue a relationship with Anne-Marie for a further year. True, mother has anxieties about whether the authorities will 'take her children away', but these seem to be remarkably easily assuaged. Anne-Marie's assertion that she is offering help to the family rather than interference appears to be accepted without cynicism. On all sides, at the root of these transactions are a set of expectations and attitudes which are increasingly unfamiliar to English child protection workers. They concern the possibility of trust in authority, trust on the part of those who possess authority that their power can be used for positive ends, and an expectation that difficulties and conflicts can be resolved through dialogue and negotiation.

By contrast, Eileen's reflections on the English case conference typify the experience of many practitioners in this country. Social workers, parents and children who are involved together in child protection work are more often than not working in a climate of fear, anxiety and hostility. If parents are apprehensive about speaking at conferences in case they 'incriminate themselves', then there are many situations in which social workers are afraid of 'getting it wrong' too. Here is part of a discussion between Brigitte, an *éducatrice* and colleague of Anne-Marie's, and Véronique who is a Children's Judge. Brigitte is trying to make sense of her English colleague's experiences:

> **Véronique:** "You had the feeling that social workers couldn't express themselves in court?"
>
> **Brigitte:** "Yes, I felt that. I had the feeling that the lawyer had considerable importance. Certainly, the social worker had explained the issues to the lawyer, the dangers to the child, but all the same it was the lawyer who spoke to the judge for the most part."
>
> **Véronique:** "So in fact, what happened was that the social worker told the lawyer about the case and he then passed it on to the judge?"
>
> **Brigitte:** "That's it, yes. I had the impression that the social worker wanted to be able to speak for herself as well, but there was a lot of anxiety for the social worker with respect to the judge. It was very striking. I had the experience of seeing my colleague working the night before at the case file, in order to be in charge of the situation in case the judge challenged her or asked questions about the case. I felt the court hearing was very, very stressful for her."

If authority relationships between social workers, families and the judiciary are different in French child protection work, then there are many reasons for this, but an important aspect of the difference is that they are *personalised*. When a Children's Judge hears a child protection case it takes the form of a discussion, and it is the judge's job not simply to implement the law but to understand the situation from as many angles as possible before reaching a decision. The same judge retains individual case responsibility for as long as any court order is in force, and most statutory orders must be reviewed by the court at regular intervals. *Éducatrices* like Anne-Marie work in close collaboration with the judge, and the quality of this working relationship is a crucial factor in their professional lives.

This personalisation in professional relationships is important in many other areas of French child protection work. One *éducatrice* was astounded at the experience of her English colleague whose case conference recommendation that a child should be rehabilitated to her mother was overruled by conference members who had never met the child. In the meeting described above by Eileen, the presence of the agency manager reflects the basic assumption that professionals should know those people about whom they take decisions, more than it represents the need for a 'senior' to be present in a managerial capacity. Clearly, when dealing with child protection issues, this idea of personalised authority cannot be about coffee and croissants and cosy chats. Far from involving the suppression of tensions, it is a way of managing the complex power relations between children, parents, social workers and the law without permanent recourse to institutionalised conflict. An *éducateur* who has worked in England for many years puts it as follows:

> "It's about a much more positive view of power than you have in social work in England. With this boy for example, I am sent there by a Children's Judge, who the kid or the family can have access to at any moment. Anyone who is unhappy, say with what their social worker has done, can phone the judge and say 'Monsieur Regnault has done this or that...' and that's a judicial process. If people don't agree with the social worker's intervention, they don't fight it out with him or her, but with the judge. They can have an hour to explain, argue, face to face with the judge, and take a lawyer if they want. There is a space – that's the important thing." (Regnault, 1994, p.45)

Regnault's idea of a space is interesting and challenging. A space for what exactly? In part, it represents the opportunity for everyone to 'have a fair hearing', a forum in which the social worker is able to speak openly and directly about their concerns. A child can if they wish speak privately with the judge, parents can remonstrate about their treatment by the social worker, and the judge can listen, debate, assess, and come to a conclusion. But is the concept of a 'fair' system, the same as that of a 'just' one? Does this way of working which seems to facilitate what we in England call 'partnership' sacrifice equally precious principles such as individual rights? The *accessibility* of the legal sphere of the French system and its *informality* when compared to our own are very seductive, but might these same characteristics not give rise to arbitrary justice and capricious judgements? These are important questions which English practitioners often asked as they struggled to reconcile their admiration and envy of French practices with their commitment to the principles underlying the English system.

The child, the family and society

French social workers, judges and families do think less about individual rights than their English counterparts and this partly explains why they do not feel uneasy with their way of working. Child protection work in France is first and foremost a *family* affair. It is not the individual child who is the primary focus of concern and intervention but the child-as-part-of-the-family and the whole thrust of the French system is towards maintaining children as part of their families of origin. Two English practitioners are discussing this:

> **Cathy:** "It's a key thing, I think the children's needs here are, well, not more important, but we look at children much more as individuals, and when looking at fostering we think about what are the child's needs whereas my impression of the French system is that they look at what's best for the family. And the individuals have to adapt. I think there's a very different view of the family's rights and those of individual members of the family."
>
> **James:** "So abuse is a family phenomenon rather than an act of violence towards an individual. That's how the system treats it."

The significance of the family as a basic unit of society and social cohesion has deep and strong roots in French history and everyday consciousness. It is also institutionalised in the French constitution and it is not unusual to hear Children's Judges quoting to families those parts of the Civil Code which speak about parents duties towards their children, and even more remarkable to English ears, children's obligations to their parents. Rousseau, the philosopher of the French Revolution wrote in the *Social Contract*:

> "So the family if you like, is the first model of a political society. The leader is the image of the father, the people are an image of the children, and they all, being born equal and free, only surrender their freedom for practical reasons." (Rousseau, 1968)

The figure of the Children's Judge was likened by some English social workers to a kind of 'super-parent', a benign authority whose wisdom is called upon when all else fails. According to this image the Judge is the concrete embodiment of the paternalistic state, which exercises both care and control. In England we tend to counterpose the family and the state, seeing the latter as somehow external to the former, but the French notion of the indivisibility of the state means that families are its constituents, and that both families and individuals belong to the state by virtue of their citizenship. So for a child to be excluded from or marginalised by its family is tantamount to its exclusion from society as a whole (Cooper 1994).

This partly helps explain why child protection work in France is not conducted in quite the same atmosphere of mistrust and persecution as in England. The *éducateur* who implements a child protection order does not represent the 'interfering state' or bureaucratic authority, in the way that English social workers can feel they do, and are presented as such by the national media. The judge, the child, parents and social workers are all members of the same state, the French Republic.

Perhaps this also explains why the atmosphere and orientation of much residential child care provision in France is very different from that of England. When Jacques, the voluntary organisation manager present at the meeting described at the start of this chapter, first visited an English children's home on a Sunday afternoon, he was shocked to find young people sitting about listening to their 'Walkmen' and looking bored. "Why aren't they out doing something, enjoying themselves?" he asked. It was close to Christmas when the authors of this book first visited a French residential training centre for young people. In the demonstration restaurant connected to the centre, which is used every day by local people, we were served a whole turkey cooked by young people in care working in the kitchens, and professionally waited on by young men and women who were also residents. A typically English reaction to this experience is to feel uncomfortable, disturbed that these young people are being exploited. In fact they are being trained, they are learning skills for their own futures. In a concrete way they are making use of an opportunity to be able to work and hence to belong to French society. Obviously, it is important not to idealise this state of affairs. Unemployment is as high in France as in England, and economic and social inequalities are rife. But around 75% of French children in residential care gain the equivalent of a City & Guilds Certificate, about 65% find employment on leaving, and overall their standard of educational attainment is no worse than for young people in day schools (Pitts 1994, Eurodata 1991). The provision and take-up of opportunities like these, and the self-evident pride of the young people in their work, represents the enactment by the state and its ordinary members of a 'social contract'. Residential provision is valued in France because it is not seen as 'residual', a last resort when all else fails, but as the continuation of parental and family provision by the state when the family itself is in difficulties.

Of course, the word for all of this is 'paternalism'. We are suspicious of paternalistic attitudes in English social work, and no doubt with justification. But there is reason to suppose that when, as in France, it is more than simply an attitude, but to all intents and purposes a structural phenomenon, a way of life that has become systematised and professionalised without losing its core meaning and value, it repays serious attention (Cooper, 1994). Here is how one English practitioner expressed it after a year of contact with France:

> "Initially I was very impressed with the close relationship between social workers and judges...but I found social workers still quite nervous about the outcome of cases with a judge making the decisions. And I began to realise that judges are very independent, and the close relationship with social workers doesn't mean that they view things entirely with a social work perspective... judges seem to bend over backwards to accommodate the parents in cases, and at the same time I think they use their authority as judges to try and force through changes by parents. So there would be a certain balance in the system. It doesn't lead to the professional abuse I would expect it to do."

We cannot just transplant deeply rooted social practices from one country to another, but we can still use them to reflect on the limitations and problems in our own way of living and working. Mrs Thatcher's famous remark notwithstanding, it is not that the idea of 'society' has disappeared from English social work and cultural consciousness, more that it is in severe tension with other trends. The following plea is still relevant to our dilemmas in the wake of the enactment of the Children Act:

> "In our view, this philosophy of partnership with clients, in which the primary caring role of the family is reasserted but effectively *supplemented* by public services, must be reintroduced into national policy and practice. The 'good society' must, in our view, treat those in need of child care services as fellow citizens rather than as 'inadequate' parents or children". (Fisher et al, 1986, p.125)

As we have suggested the notion of a 'good society' and of citizenship seems to lie at the heart of French social work practices and the society which they help sustain. However, the ideal of partnership is in many respects difficult to reconcile with the persisting emphasis in the Children Act on the rights of individuals. In principle, of course, the Act swept away the concepts of parental rights and duties and replaced them with that of 'parental responsibility'. However, the Act defines this latter concept as "All the rights, duties, powers, responsibilities and authority which by law a parent of a child has in relation to the child and his property" (CA s. 3(1)). But more significant than any definition is the manner in which the English legal system, the Act itself, and a set of dominant trends in social work culture, coalesce to legitimate formal legal competition for the *right to acquire parental responsibility*. In France, the parents of children who are the subjects of legal child protection intervention do not lose their parental rights or responsibilities, but the Children's Judge is nonetheless effectively empowered to act *in loco parentis* with respect to both children *and* parents. Individual rights are effectively subordinated to the effort to maintain family structure in the face of difficulties which threaten it.

Rights, risks and evidence – the law and social work in France and England

The profound valuation of biological family ties which underpins French society and social work practices is reflected in the limits to the powers available to social workers and judges. Children's Judges have a very wide range of statutory powers available to them, but they cannot permanently separate a child from its parents. Adoption proceedings are very rare in France by comparison with England, and take place in a different, higher court than the one in which Children's Judges hear child protection proceedings [Hetherington, R. 1993]. This has important consequences for the way all parties in child protection work experience the process. In England, when children become the subject of statutory child care proceedings, there is a high chance they will end up legally severed from their parents, adopted or in long-term fostering. Of the twelve French cases involving about 20 children which our English practitioners followed in detail, it seemed unlikely that any would be permanently separated from their parents. In the equivalent English cases, five or six children were on course to be the subjects of full care orders. At the start of the year in which comparison took place, one of the English children (Sharon Edwards) was involved in a detailed rehabilitation plan but by the end of the year she had been successfully placed for adoption.

For French families the *risks* entailed in becoming involved with the child protection system are considerably less acute than for English families. In their turn French social workers carry less of a burden of *responsibility* for the interventions they make. It is much easier for a French family than an English one to be forced to engage with the legal system, but the *consequences* are likely to be much less dramatic. This is one of the reasons why throughout our studies of French and English practitioners at work, the former seemed to experience much less *anxiety* than their colleagues here. The formal sharing of responsibility between social workers and Children's Judges adds to the French workers' sense of confidence that they are engaged in a constructive process of intervention. Here are some English practitioners' responses to watching a video of a group of *éducateurs* discussing a case:

> "They didn't seem to have to panic. A needs to be done, B needs to be done, if not we refer it to the Children's Judge, and it's all trying to get things done in a negotiated way."

> "They didn't seem concerned about the repurcussions of their decisions; they seemed to have confidence in the judge."

> "There was a willingness to involve the judicial system very early on... It almost felt to me like some of the heavy individual responsibility a social worker might carry in managing a case was not there."

French social workers do not need to obtain legally admissible evidence of abuse before they can refer a case to the judge, and equally they do not experience themselves as 'destroying families', or as having the power to do so, but as working to keep them together.

The role of 'evidence' and evidence gathering in English child protection work struck French practitioners very forcibly, and it is one key to understanding the difference between the two systems, and to thinking about how to realise the aspiration of 'partnership'. One *éducateur* had this to say:

> "What struck me the most was the split between the 'administrative' system and the judicial system where you get this pressure on the social worker at the point of taking something to court, a semi-obsession with getting evidence, a bit like a detective. In the process of gathering evidence the interests of the child seem to be rather left to one side."

In England the focus of child protection work is the duty to protect the individual child. There is a clear culture of urgency, of the need to intervene immediately and 'rescue' children from abusive situations which is not paralleled in France. The role which evidence-gathering has come to play in all phases of child protection work, but particularly during initial investigations, is a testimony to the changing balance between the influence of social work and that of the law in the total child protection endeavour (King and Piper, 1991). In order to protect individual children through the English courts social workers have increasingly come to feel that they must bend to the will of legal process and this has come to shape our entire approach to child protection work. In the collective mind of English practitioners there is now an inevitable association between intervening urgently, taking as few risks as possible, preventing further abuse, and gathering legally admissible evidence. But if a new form of practice is to emerge in the post-Children Act era, the linkages in this chain of ideas will have to be broken. Perhaps the following extracts of discussion reveal English practitioners starting to reflect that this circle does not have to remain closed for ever:

> **Eileen:** "I did a visit to a family in France – they weren't at home – but we found out from the nursery that the child had been hit that day, and there'd been a history of this, and the response was to look around for the family and to ring them later and arrange a visit next week. We would have been required by our team manager to act that day. It's not as though they weren't taking it seriously..."
>
> **James:** "There is a lack of immediacy about responding to child protection issues. We have the duty to protect, to assure ourselves that the child is protected, and that's a keynote of the initial thrust of any investigation. But in France that is not the priority. The priority seems to be to put the incident of abuse more into the context of the general family functioning. There was one sexual abuse referral and the social worker decided to act on it next week. That's inconceivable here."
>
> **Viv:** "We need to prove something that you can take to court in our system, in order to seek a supervision order or care order for example. I think within their system, because they start off possibly on a more positive basis – their philosophy is we must educate, we must clothe, we must feed the children, and if they aren't able to do that, it's more clear cut about what they should do and what they're not doing, whereas I think it's not so clear cut in this country."
>
> **Cathy:** "In this country the social work role doesn't encourage responsibility."
>
> **Viv:** "Because our system is much more adversarial than theirs, it immediately creates hostility and guilt."
>
> **Eileen:** "Well, that's the difference. Theirs is a positive statement, ours is a negative one."
>
> **Carol:** "I think it's the law. The law in France says what parents should do. The parents should educate and manage their child. When they don't, it's very clear that there's a problem and it's put in the family, and I think very often here, when a child is acting out, it's a child's problem, whereas in France it seemed to me the problem's understood to be the

family's. There's less blame, not saying, 'You are a bad parent'. They're saying 'What's happened here is that you're not managing to keep up with the law'."

Cathy: "In this country actually it almost sounds more negative in that we have to prove something is wrong, whereas maybe we should actually tackle it from the other angle – what can we do to help this family get better, rather than what can we prove is wrong in this family."

One thing which preoccupies these workers is the capacity of their French colleagues to take risks, to leave abused children in families while they assess how to intervene. French workers do experience anxiety in these situations, and they do worry about how they will be seen if something goes wrong. But they are comparatively free of one of the main sources of anxiety for English social workers, namely media vilification and the spotlight of the public enquiry and judicial condemnation. They are supported and legitimated in taking risks, not least by the partnership they have with the Children's Judge, and are freer to think about risks to *children* rather than to themselves.

It is clear that if partnership with families is to work in England, then it must be predicated on a return to a risk-taking culture in social work. The following remarks in a recent publication about implementing the Children Act are noteworthy for their effort to make this point, and their failure to grasp the wider context:

"Partnership will require decisions to be taken that may be thought by some to court trouble. Partnership, however, anticipates that risks will be taken. Inevitably there will be failures... As ever it will be social workers who will take the blame if it does not work." (Freeman 1992, p.25)

We do not propose that blame should be apportioned to any other professional group, but we do question the inevitability of a culture in which *someone* must be blamed. This is partly a matter of rethinking the relationship between power and responsibility. Any child protection system necessarily involves a variety of professions and ordinary citizens in complex and conflictual relationships, with a high chance of ambiguous or unresolved outcomes. If the structural relationships between these groupings are to various degrees weak, characterised by rigid demarcations of responsibility or power, or can be easily institutionally polarised, then blaming and scapegoating will be a feature of the system.

As the English practitioners observe in their discussion, it is in part the *adversarial* nature of English child protection law which accounts for this conflictual and blame-ridden culture. The French legal system is *inquisitorial*, and thus centrally concerned with arriving at the *truth* rather than determining *guilt*, and where English workers pursue evidence, French workers gather *information* so that the judge can arrive at *understanding*. However, while the nature of the two legal systems exerts a powerful influence on other aspects of child protection work in the two countries, there is no reason to suppose that they fully determine the surrounding system. Much of current French practice and professional philosophy contains echoes of English child protection work ten or fifteen years ago, but again there is no reason to suppose that this is because France is behind the times, just waiting for its own version of Cleveland or the Orkneys to jolt it into the future. There are examples of child protection systems, including Scotland's which are not dissimilar to that of France, and which co-habit fairly comfortably with an otherwise adversarial legal system. As Michael King and Judith Trowell point out:

> "...we are not dealing here with the difference between inquisitorial and adversarial systems, but that between systems designed to produce legal decisions and those created to interpret and deal with child protection issues as essentially family problems. It may well be that the inquisitorial system existing in continental European countries facilitated the creation of such a child and family-centred system, but there are major differences between the inquisitorial system as it applies in criminal and civil cases and the child protection jurisdiction of the Children's Judge." (1992, p.141)

Moral authority and the organisation of child protection services

In England we tend to speak of 'statutory' and 'non-statutory' services and interventions whereas in France they talk of the 'judicial' and 'administrative' spheres of the system. Although there is a clear distinction between the two levels of child protection in France, in various ways the boundary between them is more permeable than in England, and within each there is a higher degree of structural integration. In each sphere of the French system this integration coheres around a central professional figure who carries both institutional and moral authority – the Children's Judge in the judicial part of the system, and the *Inspecteur* in the administrative part. In a moment we will examine these two characters and the systems which they oversee in more detail. But first, here is a group of *éducateurs* reflecting on the relationship between the law and social work in England:

Brigitte: "I understood that in terms of the law, they have the 'Care Order' in England which seems to be very important, and gives an enormous amount of responsibility to the local authority with respect to the child. For example, the child may stay with the natural family, but if that doesn't work out, the local authority can place the child somewhere else. I have the impression that they've got big responsibilities."

Véronique: "You're saying that the child can change families without the approval of the court?"

Brigitte: "That's right. Perhaps I'm mistaken?

Véronique: "And did that seem positive or negative to you?"

Brigitte: "I'm not sure, I haven't thought about it enough."

Catherine: "I got the impression that the court has great importance at a certain point in proceedings and then after that not at all. In the case my English colleague presented to me, once a care order had been made then six months went by and the situation wasn't reviewed by the judge, and then eventually I grasped that the case wouldn't be reviewed by the court right up to when the child is 18. It really surprised me because I had the impression that the court carried enormous weight, but then I realised that social workers carry a big responsibility in terms of their work with families, and that they aren't accountable to anyone but themselves."

The separation of power and responsibility between the courts and social work in England is so much a part of life that it can come as a shock to hear others reacting to it with surprise. To French eyes the English courts and the constraints of due legal process represent a huge barrier between the 'statutory' and 'non-statutory' spheres of intervention. In the first place it is impossible to cross this barrier without the right evidence and without winning the courtroom battle. This can leave social workers with responsibility for abused children, but no power to act on their concerns. In the French way of seeing things it can leave parents with too much power. If the barrier is crossed the courts take no further active responsibility for the welfare of the child, and social workers are left with major responsibility and power in the lives of children and parents over potentially long periods of time. To French practitioners this seemed to leave parents and children with too little power, and insufficient recourse to justice. Thus, relationships between families, social workers and the judiciary in England are characterised by uneven *distributions* of power and responsibility at different points in the functioning of the system.

The Children's Judge does wield considerable power with respect to children, parents and even social workers, but the power differentials tend to remain consistent through time and the different parties have ready access to one another. One leading French judge and writer has referred to this as 'negotiated justice'. So the idea of 'personalised' authority in child protection work depends on structural features of the French way of working, on the 'open system' which families, judges and social workers find themselves working in. It also depends on power being understood to go hand in hand with responsibility. The judge does not dispense justice from a distance and wash his hands of the consequences, and when families are the subjects of statutory controls it is on the assumption that the purpose of this is to help them reassume their responsibilities. The French Children's Judge does carry ultimate responsibility for child protection cases, but in English terms this responsibility ranges over both the care and control dimensions of the work. In effect the judge is a kind of child protection case manager, combining a judicial, a therapeutic, a social and a moral function.

In so far as the judge is also at the apex of a hierarchy, commanding considerable social work and legal resources, she or he is also the hub of a *centralised* system. French families may find themselves in contact with as many if not more different professionals as an English family in similar circumstances, but the centralisation of organisational responsibility in the office of the judge, creates the possibility of effective collaboration among the range of legal, health and social work agencies which may gather around a particular child or family. This contrasts with the typical organisational picture in English child protection work, in which the task of helping people 'work together' falls less to a person or a role, than to a meeting – the case conference. If the idea of the 'key worker' represents the effort to localise responsibility in the local authority social worker, then it is instructive to compare the respective position and status of such a key worker with that of the Children's Judge. Training and experience notwithstanding, the local authority social worker occupies a fairly low position in a tall organisational hierarchy. As key worker in a child protection case she or he remains accountable to a team manager, and beyond this to more senior managers and elected politicians.

Responsible for co-ordinating multi-agency involvement, the key worker must assume formal authority with respect to more senior professionals from other disciplines. Responsibility may rest with the key worker, but power may lie in a variety of other places – with the courts, with lawyers, with social work managers, the police, and of course, with the case conference itself. *Working*

Together (HMSO, 1991) introduces the case conference as follows:

> "The conference symbolises the inter-agency nature of assessment, treatment and the management of child protection. Throughout the child protection process, the work is conducted on an inter-agency basis and the conference is the prime forum for sharing information and concerns, analysing risk and recommending responsibility for action. It draws together the staff from all the agencies with specific responsibilities in the child protection process... and provides them with the forum for conducting and agreeing their joint approach to work with the child and the family." (HMSO 1991, p.41)

Statutory child protection in France is also an inter-agency matter, but most of the key agencies operate under the direction and authority of the Children's Judge. The case conference may 'symbolise' the inter-agency nature of the work, but whether it is capable of welding the disparate parts of the total system into a coherent body is open to question. One English practitioner commented:

> "The case conference does not share anxiety, because it appoints a key worker and leaves the key worker with the anxiety. It creates a sharing of information but the key worker is the catalyst and holds the accountability and the anxiety."

One could turn this statement around and say that whereas the key worker in England is charged with case *responsibility* and in child protection work this will necessarily entail *professional anxiety*, what the individual social worker lacks is *moral and organisational authority* commensurate with both the responsibility and the anxiety they carry. The degree to which power and responsibility are structurally linked, and whether they are invested in *systems or individuals*, are key factors in how child protection functions are discharged.

The administrative sphere of the French system is also characterised by centralisation of functions and the investment of responsibility in a single individual or role. *Aide Sociale à L'Enfance* (ASE) is that section of a local authority social services department responsible for child care work, although front line practitioners are normally part of multi-disciplinary, geographically-based generic teams. The *Inspecteur* of ASE has a wide range of functions, of which the most important are the co-ordination of a multi-disciplinary child protection meeting (*Commission de Prévention*), and taking decisions about referral from the administrative sphere to the judicial. This process can be extremely rapid, and in one case observed by an English practitioner, just six days elapsed between referral to the *Inspecteur* and a judgement by the Children's Judge.

One *éducateur*, discussing the very permeable boundary between the administrative and judicial spheres in France, is led to reflect on some of its consequences:

> "On the other hand, it's true that in England the first stage in the process, before going to court, leads to a lot of thinking about how you practise with families, to the extent that in case conferences and maybe also now with the Children Act, parents participate much more... and if in France there was more collaboration with families from the start then perhaps we'd be more successful, and this would avoid what I call the systematisation, the systematic juridification of child protection in France."

Nonetheless it is clear that the French system accommodates a wide range of administrative interventions with children at risk, and in many of the cases followed by English workers there had either been long term intervention in this mode prior to judicial intervention, or a combination of judicial and administrative orders in families with more than one child, or cases were being successfully contained within a purely administrative framework. To some degree the formal mode of intervention in this domain, the *AEMO administrative*, can be compared to an English intervention under the auspices of the child protection case conference. However, there are important differences. A referral to the *Commission d'Prévention* may not imply such a high level of anxiety and concern as would the convening of a case conference. Following the implementation of an *AEMO administrative*, case responsibility will often remain with the local authority multidisciplinary team rather than being referred to the specialist services which implement judicial orders. Finally, as well as taking decisions about the type of action to be taken, the *Inspecteur* has decision-making powers with respect to a wide range of resources which can be mobilised to support the family.

In comparable non-statutory and administrative cases, English practitioners will be talking about *child protection* while their French counterparts will refer to *action éducative*. Formal administrative intervention in the French system is framed in terms of a package of support and *éducation*, and while surveillance may be involved it is not the central concern. Increasingly in England the case conference system has become annexed to the domain of statutory intervention, frequently being a prelude to judicial interventions, there being no clear systemic boundary between those cases which belong in the 'preventative' domain and those in the 'statutory' domain. Writing about the blurred boundary beween case conferences and court proceedings, David Storr comments:

> "In reality, conferences can easily become kangaroo courts. Their findings may not be of fact or guilt, but they can be of similar significance – impinging as they do on family relationships, social acceptance and even employment... A fundamental question is 'What is a case conference?' Widely referred to as if they are clearly defined entities, in reality they are not." (Storr 1994, p.6)

In France, while there is the capacity for rapid and fluid movement between the administrative and judicial spheres of intervention, it is clear that there is an extensive domain of preventative work which, while it is in effect concerned with 'child protection', is still clearly demarcated from judicial intervention.

Individualism and collectivism – the politics of practice

Child protection practices cannot but reflect and be shaped by the wider society of which they are a part, although they also help to reproduce that broader social and political context. Contemporary English society is powerfully shaped by ideologies of political and social individualism. By contrast, French society since the revolution of 1789 and the creation of the first Republic is firmly rooted in collectivist principles. To some extent social work in England has been part of an oppositional tendency, with strong links to left wing and minority political cultures of various sorts. But comparison with France reveals how modern social work radicalism in England is still shaped by individualistic, pluralist, and liberal ideas which are largely foreign to the republican spirit.

The *holistic* tendencies of French child protection work – the emphasis on family as opposed to individual functioning, on social *'inclusion'* as an extension of family membership, and on universal standards of acceptable behaviour – are reinforced by the structure of the child protection system which integrates the social work and legal functions and centralises authority in key figures who embody the interests of *both* the family *and* the state. English ideologies stress the rights of individuals, the autonomy and 'difference' of minority groupings, and in general the separation of state and civil life. These differences even affect the way a case conference functions when compared with an *audience* with the

Judge or a meeting of the *Commission de Prévention*. Consistent with an adversarial legal culture, participants at a case conference are invited to come and put their case or argue their point of view. Parents who are unwilling to attend or speak at a conference might be respected partly on the grounds that they are exercising a *right* to silence. But the Children's Judge or *Inspecteur* interviewing a family, *expects* that his or her questions will be answered in return for the opportunity afforded to the child or parent to speak in their turn. This expectation will normally be met because of the shared assumption that ultimately everyone shares the same interests.

English and French practitioners experienced considerable difficulty assimilating each other's practice ideologies with respect to ethnic minorities and oppressed or marginal groupings. This was the arena in which differences between the two working cultures appeared most acute, as though a collision of fundamental world views had occurred. The republican universalism which informs French practice is clearly evident in how this *éducateur* thinks about the question of working with north African 'immigrant' families:

> "I think that a north African battered child is suffering as much as a French child. At this level of difficulty it's universal not cultural. From the moment these families arrive in France they have to be warned of their rights and duties, it's a whole thing that north African families have to integrate. It's true that cultural difference complicates the understanding of the case, but it's also true that for myself I say, 'In France, there are French laws'."

There are strong echoes here of the social and professional attitudes, described earlier, which inform the stance of Children's Judges, *Inspecteurs*, and the functioning of the entire French system. The moral confidence which underlies such a stance towards what in England we would describe as a 'black family' derives partly from France's relationship with its former colonies. Consistent with the republican ethic the inhabitants of these colonies were granted French citizenship, an important political concession never conferred by Her Majesty's governments on the 'subject' populations of the British Empire. Politically and constitutionally the majority of ethnic minority inhabitants of France are *French*, and it was a source of surprise to English practitioners that this was how they wished to see themselves. The French concept of *'inclusion'*, of belonging to society, is closely tied to that of *'intégration'*. As Dominique Schnapper (1992, p.114) observes, France is "the nation-state par excellence and as a result the nation of individual integration." And so, he continues:

> "...a politics which aims at the integration of individuals cannot but be 'colour blind': particular measures (to address the needs of ethnic groups) are seen as discriminatory." (1992, p.118)

This is not a whimsical matter, but deeply rooted in the political history of France and some other European countries. Writing about France, Germany and the Netherlands, Robert Miles (1993) makes the point that for French governments of the 1980s *'intégration individuelle'* was part of the solution to racism. So also,

> "A Race Relations Act (of which there have been three in Britain since the mid-1960s) is inconceivable in these three countries because it would be instantly and widely interpreted as legislation intended to regulate relations between different 'races' in a manner that echoes the 'final solution' to the 'Jewish problem'." (1993, p.20)

Reflecting this, the anxiety which some aspects of the politics of English social work practice occasions for French workers can be detected in the reflections of this *assistante sociale*:

> "What I picked out was the importance given to ethnic origin, giving priority to social workers of the same ethnic background as the clients they were working with, which might be a positive difference in their system, but I think it's debatable since it tends towards a situation in which ethnic groups aren't mixing, having children's homes and other institutions with ethnic groups and staff of the same race, not a mixture, and that shocked me."

Whether or not this practitioner has accurately understood the intended outcomes of English policy and practice, French workers were equally shocked by same race placement policies which they saw as running completely counter to any philosophy of 'anti-racism' or 'integration', and remarked that North African families frequently request foster placements with white families in order to promote integration.

In their turn English practitioners were disturbed to encounter a practice in which attention to the specific cultural needs of ethnic minority families took its place *alongside* a range of other criteria for assessing interventions rather than attracting priority. One practitioner who had opportunities to look at French community prevention projects commented like this:

> "Certainly, around gender there was no work happening on

the estate with girls and young women which is very different from what we are doing in my area. The whole issue of racism was extremely uncomfortable for me, it just wasn't addressed as much as it should be... A lot of kids who come there are of North African background, but there is very little representation of that in the project. I guess I entered this research thinking the spirit of work with children in the community would be much more progressive – given their *liberté, égalité, fraternité* – but I came away thinking that they're not half way down the road that we are in the agency I work with."

From the perspective of French collectivist and holistic practices, the English emphasis on respecting and confirming the social identity of a range of separate marginalised or disadvantaged groups constitutes a kind of political fragmentation. "In England the structures are splintered," said the counterpart of the worker quoted above. "Each person has responsibility for a particular area – adolescents, children, drug users, old people..." By contrast, the key French categories in this respect are generic, *inclusion* and *exclusion*, and the political dimension of French practice concerns the situation of *les exclus* whoever they may be. The right of *every* individual to the benefits of citizenship is what *liberté, égalité, fraternité* are understood to confer. Thus poverty as a mode of social marginalisation remains at the centre of political and social work discourse in France, serving as an uncomfortable reminder of those categories and people who have been largely eclipsed by the 'identity politics' of the last decade in English social work.

The analysis of *political* cultures outlined above is not, of course, confined to questions of race, gender, class or any other social category. As we hope this chapter has made clear, it must be central to the understanding of the entire social work or child protection endeavour within any culture or nation. To reflect on possibilities for professional change is a project which must incorporate awareness of the limits of one's own social world. Contact with another culture, where 'the same problems' are conceptualised and acted on very differently, and are consequently not really quite 'the same problems', leads us to realise that we *make* the social and interpersonal world we inhabit as professionals and ordinary citizens. With time, thought, and will we can also remake our worlds according to a different set of purposes.

This book focuses in detail on some possibilities for remaking our child protection system, not necessarily in the image of France or any other country. Rather, through receptivity to a different way of seeing and doing things, we hope to point to some alternative futures for ourselves.

Chapter 2: Resources and Benefits for Families in Need in France and England

In the following chapter, we consider the type and nature of resources and benefits typically available to four comparable fictional families, two from each country.

The Matthews, our first English family, comprise the mother Anne, the step-father Ian and four children: John 14, Mark 11, Theresa 6 and Susie 12 months. This family can be compared with Philippe and Danielle Bertillon, a French couple with three children: Michelle 13, Aude 7 and Louis 12 months old. The Lewis's, the other English family, comprise the mother, Jane, and her two children, Sally 16, and Katy 4. They can be compared with the Picot family, of whom Marie-Claude is the mother with two children, Jean 15, and André 5.

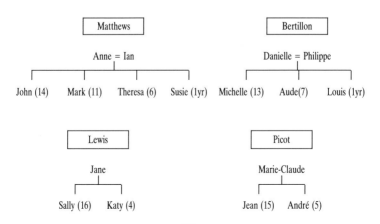

Income support

First we consider the state benefits that are available, and the economic position in which the four families are likely to find themselves as a result.

Whereas Philippe is working, Ian is not. Ian's benefits, income support, unemployment benefit, hardship grants, crisis loans, and so on, have their origins in the Beveridge reforms of the immediate post-war period in England. Beveridge was concerned to create a universal system of social security in which everyone was guaranteed a minimum income "sufficient to keep them above want" (Chamberlyne 1991). This model has at its centre a traditional family, with the father in full time employment and the mother performing the childcare tasks at home (Chamberlyne 1991).

France has a family policy in which there are financial incentives to families to procreate. Following the First World War, *allocations de maternité* for mothers under 25 having their first child, or to any child born within the first year of marriage were instituted (Ashford 1988).

The law of 22nd August 1946 regularised family benefits: family allowance, maternity grants and housing benefit, as well as creating a more generous benefit and tax relief system for families, especially those with several children (Hantrais 1994, Neubauer 1992).

This means that the Picots, with their two children, will receive a larger addition to their family income than the Lewis's, and this difference is even greater for the Bertillons relative to the Matthews because they have a larger family.

The Lewis's and the Picots, as single parent families, represent the family groupings which do not fall into the family ideal upon which the English Welfare State was based. The number of single parent families in both countries has increased markedly in recent years. Currently, 16% of French families and 22% of English families are headed by a single parent (Eurostats 1994). In both countries, single parent families are the most impoverished (Kamerman 1984). In France, if Marie-Claude were not working, she might receive an income similar to the average wage for production workers (Bryson 1992). This could include single parent benefit, which in itself reflects a difference in attitude between France and England (Commaille 1994). In England, Jane with her two children would be part of the 32% of the population whose income is less than the median.

Child care benefits and child care services

So what financial child care benefits are available to our families? Anne gave up her job to have her youngest child, and for this she would have had maternity benefit, at a rate of 90% of earnings for the first 6 weeks, a flat rate for 12 weeks and nothing for the rest of the time (Cohen 1993). Danielle, who did the same thing having had her third child, was entitled to 16 weeks maternity leave at 84% of her earnings which was untaxed. She is also entitled to parental leave for the first 36 months of the child's life, and, as she has just had her third child, she is also entitled to a flat rate payment which in 1991 was the equivalent of just over £300 a month. The measures taken in the 1980s in France were designed to enable mothers to work and have a family more easily, and the overall package of child allowances in France is one of the most generous in Europe (Hantrais 1994).

In France, child care costs are tax-deductible. In Anne's case, childcare is only tax deductible if it is workplace based (Chamberlyne 1991). As an English single mother, Jane's plight is only now being recognised. At the time of writing the government has stated its intention to introduce a £40 allowance towards childcare costs for single parents.

What is the level of child care provision for pre-school children? André, at 5, would be one of the 95% of 3–6 year olds who could attend a French state-run nursery. Katy, at 4, would be one of only 35% who have access to publicly funded nursery provision in England. However, this provision is increasingly used for children who are at risk, as is the 2% of state provision for 0 to 3 year olds.

The extensive child care provision in France has its origins in French family policy in which families and children are viewed as the building blocks of society. In England by contrast, child care has traditionally been viewed as a mother's responsibility and so the state has not attempted to make a comprehensive service available. Until relatively recently in England, mistrust of day care facilities for children was fairly widespread. There was a view that separation from the mother was emotionally damaging (Cannan 1992). In the last century, day centres were established on the model of the French crèche, only to founder through the misgivings of the mothers themselves (Bryson 1992).

The hours that childcare is available also dictate the nature and duration of the work that a mother can undertake. In France, 40-hour-a-week day care is universally available, whereas in England full-time provision is much rarer: in only 15% of places. Not surprisingly, whereas 40% of French mothers with children under 10 work full time, less than 20% of English mothers do (Hantrais

1994). Despite the paucity of child care provision, a greater number of English women are working than ever before (Moss 1987). However, much of this increase is accounted for by part-time work.

The main alternative to nursery school for working mothers is childminding. Like England, France has a registered childminder service. There has been an enormous increase in registered childminding in England in the last three decades. Whereas childminding in England used to be seen as the poor families' option, it is now far more widely used (Moss 1987). It is difficult to know how extensive the use of unregistered childminding is. France has an established network of childminders linked to the social services organisation, the PMI, which is concerned with the needs of all children and their mothers up to the age of 6. In France there are 50,000 childminders who care for about 60,000 children (Hetherington et al 1993). In addition, each PMI employs a number of *'assistante maternelles'*, who are a cross between a foster care worker and a childminder and work with families deemed to have special needs.

What kind of facilities will be open to Anne and Danielle whilst they look after Susie and Louis at home? Both mothers will still be receiving post natal care. In France these clinics are run by the PMI. For the child's first year of life, the mother will probably attend monthly, and thereafter she can attend six-monthly until the child is six (Girodet 1990). Alternatively the health visitor can visit the child in need at home, and in some cases visits can take place two or three times a week. In contrast, in England regular visiting after the first few weeks of life tends to be limited to those who are at risk and visits are still only likely to take place about once a month.

Child protection: detection and monitoring

The health visitors at the clinics of both Susie Matthews and Louis Bertillon notice bruising. At the moment the level of supervision of both is about the same, so this is picked up simultaneously. At this point, in France, the system for discovering and monitoring child abuse is already in place, as the PMI, to which the family clinic service belongs, has as its other remit specialist work with deprived families and those with severe difficulties (Hetherington et al 1993). It has at its disposal nurses, midwives, paediatricians, and nursery nurses. In addition to the PMI, the local authority social work department *(DISS – Direction des Interventions Sanitaires et Sociales)* also has under its aegis general social work services and Children's Services (ASE). These three services join

Figure 1

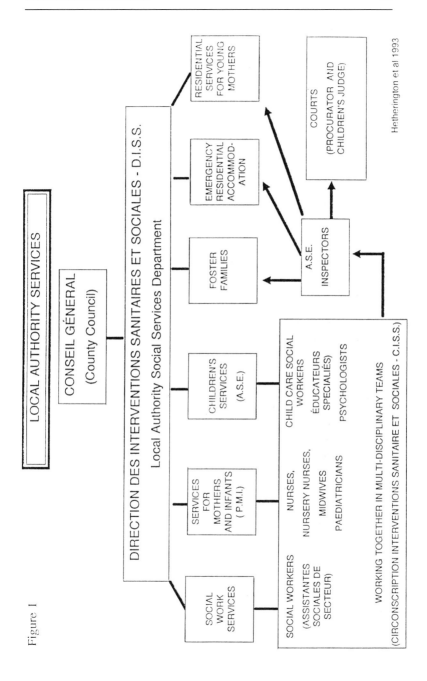

Hetherington et al 1993

together to form multi-disciplinary teams containing: *assistants sociaux de secteur*, who are the nearest equivalent to local authority social workers; *éducateurs*, who are concerned with child and family development; and psychologists (see Fig 1). These teams, which cover a geographical area, are subordinate to the local authority called the *Circonscription (CISS)*. Therefore, French families will have a wide range of professions already available to work with them. On the other hand, the English health visitor, who is a part of the National Health Service, will have to refer a child to a local authority Social Services Department.

Staff at the *école maternelle* (nursery school) run by the PMI attended by André Picot notice that he is bruised and dirty and that his attendance is sporadic. They report this to the ASE. It is only because of her dealings with Sally on another matter that the social worker notices that Katy is withdrawn and behaving very strangely. This cannot be picked up at nursery school because, due to a shortage of provision, Katy cannot attend one.

The older children start manifesting behavioural problems at school. John Matthews becomes disruptive, and on occasions he is violent and abusive to teachers. Sally Lewis, starts playing truant and behaving badly at school. The teachers therefore contact both the local authority Social Services Department and the Educational Welfare Service. Theresa starts behaving in a sexually provocative manner and the school nurse is concerned about some marks she finds during a routine medical examination. Aude blurts out to her friend that she is being sexually abused, which worries the teacher who overhears it. In these cases the schools inform the local authority social services (CISS).

At the same time, Theresa is rushed to hospital with a fracture, and confides to a nurse that she is being sexually abused. The nurse, under a statutory obligation to inform social services, does so. Aude is taken ill and she also confides in medical staff, although she subsequently denies everything. This is not reported to the social services, but they already have the information from Aude's teacher.

Marie-Claude, who has previously spent some time in a home for young mothers run by the PMI, now works in a factory. She is having problems coping with the daily running of the home and with her children. She therefore goes to see the factory social worker. She could have seen the *assistant social de secteur* or referred herself directly to the Children's Judge to deal with the problems with her children. The factory social worker refers her to the ASE.

The Matthews' next door neighbours do not like the way the children are being treated, and phone the Social Services Department to report them. The neighbours toy with the idea of not leaving their name, but decide that they will. This type of referral is a much less common occurrence in France.

Family services: prevention or cure?

The *assistante sociale* of the ASE to whom Marie-Claude Picot was referred has gone to see the family. She feels that it would be appropriate to bring in a *family aide* to help with daily household matters, with the aim of assisting the family to manage on its own. The *assistante sociale* also feels that the mother needs some help with budgeting, so she asks for a *tutelle* who may either be employed by the DISS or the *Caisse Assistance Familiale*, the organisation responsible for administering Family Allowances. This contrasts with England, where family budgeting is more likely to be regarded as beyond the remit of child protection work. An English practitioner has commented that in France there seems to be more support and help towards rehabilitation.

Because of the problems with Louis Bertillon, the *assistante sociale* feels that the family should go to the CMPP *(Centre Medico Psycho-Pedagogic)*, a voluntary agency similar to a child and family guidance clinic. The help the family will receive here is psychotherapeutic. Alternatively, Louis could have attended a child and family guidance centre run by the PMI.

The services available to the family, both universal and specialist, are oriented to *éducation* and prevention. This is very different from the situation in England.

But why, and in what ways are they so different? The first major difference is ideological and is rooted in the assumption that the French State should assume an active role in encouraging all citizens to use public services in order that they receive adequate *éducation* (Cannan 1992). It therefore makes very generous provision for its *éducatif* services. In England, the privacy of the family is a paramount value and the state may only interfere when things go wrong. Consequently, more universal services are provided in France, and a greater number of these are for *éducation* and preventative purposes and are aimed at the whole family. On the other hand, in England aid is concentrated on families in need, tending to focus upon the children rather than the adults.

As a result of the preventative, *éducative* orientation of French family policy, it is written into the law that the local authority has a duty to provide preventative projects in areas of social deprivation. To fulfil this, the local authority often contracts out to voluntary agencies which provide specialist child care services. An example of such a project is the after-school centre in Beauvais, where children of families with problems can obtain social work support and help with homework. It also runs cultural and recreational activities for families.

Voluntary and statutory intervention

It becomes apparent that André's social and emotional development is at risk. After a meeting with the ASE, he is placed on an administrative AEMO *(Action Educative en Milieu Ouvert)*. An AEMO is a measure usually administered by a multi-disciplinary team from a voluntary agency. This team is contracted to work with the family for a fixed length of time and for a specific purpose. These agencies can be contracted either by the *inspecteur* of the ASE (administrative AEMO) or by the Children's Judge (judicial AEMO). For an administrative AEMO to be established, the parents must cooperate with the workers. In André's case a contract is established with a voluntary organisation providing an AEMO service to his local authority and the local Children's Judges.

Voluntary agencies play a more significant role in the French child protection system (Bullock 1993). Rather than providing supplementary services to the statutory sector, French voluntary agencies carry formal responsibility for key aspects of child protection. The services of French voluntary agencies are utilised on a contractual basis by social services and the Children's Judge.

In England, the division between voluntary and statutory provision means that, in general, non-statutory services attract the less contentious cases. This contrasts with France, where complex, high risk cases are routinely referred on to the AEMO team by the judge or the *Inspecteur.*

Access to resources: multi-disciplinary teams versus individual professionals

Let us return now to the Lewis's. Katy's development is believed to be suffering, and so a referral is made to a play therapist. While there are no play therapists as such in the French system, a similar role is discharged by the *éducatrice*. The *éducatrice* is a type of social worker which does not exist in England, and carries special responsibility for direct work with children and young people.

It is also felt that Katy needs the services of a psychologist. In England, this would necessitate a further referral, the costs of which would be balanced against other demands upon the social service's budget. In reality of course, the English social worker would probably be expected to do the job themselves. The English social workers involved in our study gained the impression that in France, psychologists play a central role in the multi-disciplinary team and they were envious of the fact that this was a resource routinely available to social workers. André, for example, has the services not only of a psychologist in the CISS, but also in the CMPP that he attends.

The search for resources is time consuming especially if there is no guarantee that they will be available. A French practitioner commented that English social workers are "always running around looking for resources". This need, to locate specialist resources anew each time, contrasts markedly with the situation in France in which a broad range of resources are already there as an established part of the package.

Nevertheless, resources still have to be obtained from outside the French multi-disciplinary team. The use of the equivalent of child and family guidance clinics or assistance with schooling (a *soutien scholaire*) has to be cleared by the *Inspecteur* of the ASE in the same way as senior management in English Social Services Departments have to approve requests for resources. The fact that there are fewer requests increases the chance that any particular application will be successful, however. Moreover, the purchaser-provider split which is prevalent in English social work now entails a greater emphasis upon the search for facilities and resources.

The law and resources

As we have seen, there were strong suspicions that both Aude and Theresa had been sexually abused. Theresa's situation offers a useful illustration of the impact of the English preoccupation with abuse on the use of resources. Social workers engaged with Theresa's family would be using their time to gather evidence in order to bring a case to court. In the view of some practitioners, this accounts for the biggest drain on resources in child protection social work. One of them summed up the situation thus:

> "The social work aspect has gone ... The resources that are there are diverted into legal procedures. The resources are greater than they were 19 years ago. And yet 19 years ago I was able to do more social work than I can now. Then I could do a report on what's going on, the dynamics, why we think things are happening, rather than a factual account of events that you could put before the magistrates who say the case is proved and that I must make an order."

"Everything is being gobbled up in procedures. You're wasting time bringing in the child protection team – I say wasting time because 50% of the time when we have involved them, the case doesn't amount to anything legal. We're wasting time in procedures that aren't helping the child; aren't particularly helping the family very much or the social worker. And yet there's all this work going on. Perhaps it's about lawyers and barristers having more to argue with. At the end of the day what the legal department says is more important than what I learnt in the CQSW. That's what's consuming our resources and stopping us doing real imaginative work with families."

At this point, English social workers would probably be working towards a case conference, which would place the child on the child protection register thus releasing previously unavailable resources. In England, child care resources are increasingly targeted at children at risk. In one English case, a particular health service resource for a boy with severe behavioural difficulties only became available after he was placed on the register.

In Aude's case, the legal proceedings, being inquisitorial rather than adversarial, did not require legally admissible evidence of abuse. The social workers merely need to satisfy themselves that there is serious cause for concern about the family. There would be no need for a social services department to employ lawyers. There would be a meeting chaired by the *Inspecteur* of the ASE, where the professionals involved with the family would be present. The *Inspecteur* would then decide whether or not the case should be referred via the procurator to the Children's Judge.

The Children's Judge is responsible for both young offenders and children in moral or physical danger. His meetings are informal and he can be approached by the parents, the child or the ASE via a Procurator. The Procurator is the person who determines whether cases should go to court.

The judges have a number of measures at their disposal (see Fig. 2). They can refer the case to a separate child care service for an investigation. This service is called the COAE (*Consultation d'Orientation et d' Action Educative*). Alternatively, they could send the child to the welfare service (*Service Educatif auprès du Tribunal pour Enfants*), which normally happens in the case of young offenders (see Fig. 2). Alternatively, he could impose a care order on the child, enabling the social workers to place it in a residential establishment or foster placement. In Aude's case, however, the aim is to obtain a judicial AEMO, in order to impress on the parents the severity of the situation and to require

Figure 2

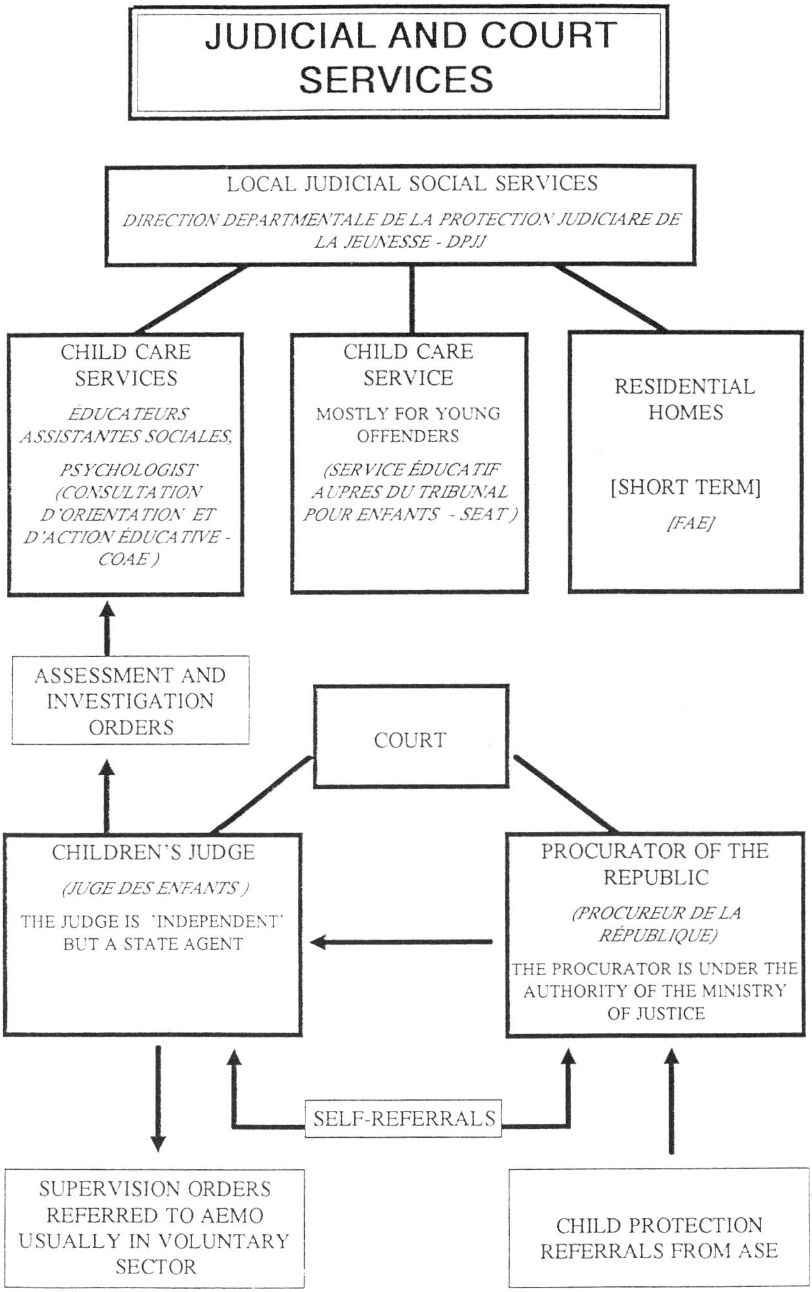

JUDICIAL AND COURT SERVICES

LOCAL JUDICIAL SOCIAL SERVICES

DIRECTION DEPARTMENTALE DE LA PROTECTION JUDICIARE DE LA JEUNESSE - DPJJ

CHILD CARE SERVICES

EDUCATEURS ASSISTANTES SOCIALES,

PSYCHOLOGIST (CONSULTATION D'ORIENTATION ET D'ACTION ÉDUCATIVE - COAE)

CHILD CARE SERVICE

MOSTLY FOR YOUNG OFFENDERS

(SERVICE ÉDUCATIF AUPRES DU TRIBUNAL POUR ENFANTS - SEAT)

RESIDENTIAL HOMES

[SHORT TERM]

[FAE]

ASSESSMENT AND INVESTIGATION ORDERS

COURT

CHILDREN'S JUDGE

(JUGE DES ENFANTS)

THE JUDGE IS 'INDEPENDENT' BUT A STATE AGENT

PROCURATOR OF THE REPUBLIC

(PROCUREUR DE LA RÉPUBLIQUE)

THE PROCURATOR IS UNDER THE AUTHORITY OF THE MINISTRY OF JUSTICE

SELF-REFERRALS

SUPERVISION ORDERS REFERRED TO AEMO USUALLY IN VOLUNTARY SECTOR

CHILD PROTECTION REFERRALS FROM ASE

Hetherington et al 1993

them to cooperate. There is no evidence of abuse, just a clear
indication that there is something seriously wrong in the family.
Once the AEMO is imposed, the key worker would be the
éducateur of the AEMO team, although the *assistant social de
secteur* and the *éducatrice de CISS* would still be working with the
girl.

In Theresa's case, the local authority social worker has
assembled sufficient legally admissible evidence for the department's legal section to support taking the case to court. However,
as an English social worker observed, after the expenditure of all
this time and all these resources:

> "You have this wonderful procedure, and you get this section
> 8 order, and all these wonderful things, and everybody goes
> away, and what have you got left? You've got the family, the
> child and the social worker, the same people as you had in the
> beginning, all trying to make sense of the new relationship..."

Educational problems

Sally's behaviour at school is getting worse. She is playing truant
more and more and is obviously very disturbed. She is also
reacting badly to the situation at home. The social workers decide
to send Sally to a Day Assessment Unit to help her reintegrate into
the school. It is not long before Sally is ready to return to
mainstream education, but because of her prior problems, some
schools refuse to take her. In France, schools are not allowed to
refuse children.

Michelle Bertillon also refuses to go to school, and the school
informs the social workers. When the *assistante sociale* fails to get
the girl's cooperation, she asks to see the Children's Judge, who
sets up an *Orientation en Milieu Ouvert*. This is undertaken by
Consultation d'Orientation Educative, an assessment body
attached to the court. In this team there is an *éducatrice* who works
with Michelle to plan her return to school, and a psychologist who
works with the mother.

We recall that John Matthews had very serious behavioural
problems at school. He was eventually excluded because of these.
In the short term, John had home tuition from a special needs
teacher. He was at the beginning of his GCSE years, but the
teacher available was not qualified in the subjects he was taking.
She was also only available for a limited number of hours in the
week.

John was later sent to a boarding school for emotionally and
behaviourally disturbed children, as a weekly boarder. About 40%

of all children in residential care in England are at one of these schools (Colton and Hellinckx 1993). Many of them are privately run, by a variety of trusts and other organisations ranging from businesses to statutory bodies. School fees are usually paid by the Education Authority, although a high proportion of residents are jointly funded by Social Services Departments and Education Authorities. According to the staff of one school, referrals are received from social workers daily, but many of them founder due to lack of resources. Staffing at the schools can vary markedly, from those who employ fully qualified social workers only, to those who train inexperienced staff 'on the job'. Education tends to take second place to the care and containment of young people's behaviour and these schools therefore tend to act as a holding agent until the child is legally able to leave school.

In France, Jean begins to have behavioural problems and experiences increasing difficulty relating to his mother, who cannot cope with him. He is also disruptive at school although not enough to be excluded. The *assistant social* senses how serious matters have become and asks him what he would like to do for a career – he is 15. He decides that he would like to be a chef, and so the *assistant social* asks if he would like to go to one of the nationwide network of residential training centres for children and young people from disturbed and deprived backgrounds. At this centre there is an entrance exam, and the residents are taught a trade and study for vocational qualifications. There is good social work back-up at the centre, which is staffed by *éducateurs*. It is available for young people up to the age of 21. Jean takes pride in the fact that he has been offered a place there and is therefore more motivated to do well. If he does not perform adequately he will have to leave. This centre is one of five providing vocational training for youngsters with problems in his area.

Psychiatric and health service provision

It becomes apparent that Mark needs psychiatric help and is being rejected by his parents. The reluctance to have children psychiatrically assessed in England and the lack of psychiatric facilities for youngsters was not apparent in France. Since the Second World War social work in France has been strongly influenced by psychiatry (Corbillon 1991, Chauvière 1980), and this was demonstrated by the fact that at least some of the children in our study lived in psychiatric units administered by EMP (*Externa Medico-Psychiatric*) or IME (*Institut Medico-Educative*). However, it appears that the availability of psychiatric services in France is variable. One of the French practitioners commented that if a family is being seen by a psychologist the psychiatrist is unlikely to become involved, and that there are still large areas of France without psychiatric services.

Fostering, adoption or residential care?

Theresa's social worker has now obtained an Emergency Protection Order and placed her in a short term foster placement. Following this, the court imposes a care order, and Theresa is again fostered. The French practitioners commented favourably on the well established system and good range of crisis, medium term and long term care that is available in England, as an alternative to a residential placement.

Susie is also placed on the child protection register because of the marks that were found on her, and more worryingly that she had a sister who is in care as a result of sexual abuse. Once the requisite evidence is obtained, the social workers request a care order, and she is placed in foster care with a view to adoption. The process of adoption in England – advertising and calling in private foster care agencies at up to £25,000 a time when social services departments fostering and adoption units are unable to find families – is an enormous drain on resources.

At the same time, the *assistant social* dealing with Louis Bertillon because of the bruising, has decided that the child should be removed from home. For reasons which will become clear later in this book, it is very unlikely that the child would be put up for adoption. To remove the child from home, the social services must go to the Children's Judge. One-year-old Louis is placed in a *pouponnière*, a home for very small children.

The prevalence of residential care in France, as opposed to foster care and adoption, stems from cultural attitudes towards the family. In England, by contrast the debate about the damaging effects of residential care has precipitated a dramatic shift towards fostering in recent years. This difference is reflected in the fact that in France 52% of children in care are fostered, whilst in England the figure is 67% (Colton and Hellinckx 1993).

Overview

Figure 3 identifies the services that have been utilised by or for each of our fictional families.

The most striking feature about these lists of professionals is that a French family is likely to have many more services or individual professionals working with it than an English family. There are four main reasons for this: different philosophies and policies vis a vis the family; a different mix of, and relationship between, voluntary and statutory provision in the child protection system; the organisation of service delivery on the basis of multidisciplinary teams rather than individual professional practice; and the increasing influence of legal and managerial imperatives upon professional practice in the English child protection system.

The level of resources available to families in the English child protection system is determined by the traditional English commitment to non-intervention in the family. In France, by contrast, there are far more *éducatif* and preventative programmes available. When a case comes to the ASE, there are far more options at its disposal, and according to the English social workers there are "more people available, more help and more avenues to be pursued in the French system."

As the majority of services are provided by the local authority social worker in England, the same person may well be responsible for following cases from start to finish. This means that fewer professionals are involved at the different stages in a family's progress through the system. In contrast, as we have seen, French families may well be referred into an AEMO team from the voluntary sector and they will therefore have an input from both voluntary and statutory multi-disciplinary teams.

The existence of these multi-disciplinary teams in France means that both clients and workers have ready access to a far broader range of specialisms and so, to greater expertise. There is, therefore, less competition for a limited budget. In contrast, English local authority social workers have to apply for each resource separately and this leads to inconsistency and time wasting. As an English social worker remarked: "Resources are easy to identify, but hard to come by."

Whereas, in England, there are many different professionals involved, as was the case with Theresa's family, many of them will be exclusively concerned with detection, investigation and legal matters. This has had a significant effect on the distribution of resources. English child protection agencies, voluntary and statutory, are spending an increasing amount of time on monitoring children in danger in their quest for evidence, rather than doing social work with them. They are also making services available to those deemed to be at risk or in need of protection to the detriment of those with equally pressing, but less legally clear cut, problems. French social workers, untroubled by the need to assemble legally admissible evidence, are able to put most of their time and resources into child protection social work.

Figure 3.

Matthews

Anne = Ian
LA social worker

John (14)	Mark (11)	Theresa (6)	Susie (1yr)
teacher	LA social worker	LA social worker	LA social worker
LA social worker		LA team manager	LA team manager
special needs teacher		school nurse	health visitor
special school teachers		teacher	LA solicitor
and social workers		hospital nurse	judge
		social work child	social work child protection
		protection team	team
		police child protection	police child protection
		team	team
		social work lawyers	foster mother
		judge	LA fostering and adoption
		foster mother	team social workers
		LA fostering and	private fostering and
		adoption team social	adoption team
		workers	
		psychologist	

Bertillon

Danielle = Philippe
Assistant social de secteur

Michelle (13)	Aude (7)	Louis (1yr)
teacher	CISS (ASE) team:–	PMI (CISS) health clinic
CISS (ASE) team:–	assistant social de secteur	PMI (CISS team:–
assistant social de secteur	éducatrice	psychologist
éducatrice	psychologist	paediatrician
psychologist	inspecteur	éducatrice
inspecteur	AEMO team:–	assistant social
COAE team:–	éducateur	pouponnière
psychologist	psychologist	éducatrices
éducatrice		CMPP team:–
judge		psychologists
independent agency help with		éducatrices
schooling		
AEMO team (JCLT):–		
éducateur		
psychologist		

Lewis

Jane

Sally (16)

teacher
Educational Welfare Officer
LA social worker
day assessment unit

Katy (4)

family centre social worker
LA social worker
play therapist
psychologist

Picot

Marie-Claude

home for young mothers
family aide
tutelle

Jean (15)
special training school:–
   éducatrice
   teacher

André (5)
ASE:–
   psychologist
   éducatrice
   assistant social de secteur;
PMI école maternelle:–
   assistante maternelle
AEMO team of (voluntary agency)–
   psychologist
   éducatrice

Section Two
Working Together

Chapter 3: Entering the French Child Protection System

How do things work out for those involved in child protection when the system is based on welfare not rights? When the judge is not an arbitrator but the representative of the victim? When it is difficult (and rare) for a child to be permanently separated from its family of origin? The following chapters consider what happens to families and social workers when the family becomes involved with social workers over problems of their children's upbringing.

If we had wanted to make an analysis of the English cases in our study we would have used headings like 'investigation of child abuse', 'assessment' and 'monitoring', and 'the role of the legal system'. These categories seemed, in relation to the French cases, irrelevant and confusing. It was more enlightening to look at what happened if the family was co-operative and what happened if the family was not co-operative. Although the cases will show this was something of an over-simplification, we found it to be a helpful distinction. Another way of categorising the material would be to consider the bureaucratic systems involved. One could divide the French system into three components; the services of the CISS which offers the basic social work provision available to all, the services of Aide Sociale a l'Enfance, ASE, which provides a specialist service for children, and the judicial system. The first two cases that we describe in this chapter demonstrate why this is not as helpful as it sounds, and why even the broad issue of co-operation or non co-operation is not entirely satisfactory either. The French cases flow between different parts of the system, while taking with them accretions from different aspects of the system that they have been in touch with, like sticks caught in the eddies of a leisurely river; English cases proceed more briskly down a controlled and channelled waterway, occasionally interrupted or redirected by a legal weir.

The French and English social workers in our project agreed on many things; they had similar views on what constituted child abuse; and they used similar conceptual frameworks for understanding human growth and development. They all used systemic concepts to understand families and organisations, and, to a varying degree, used these ideas in their work. They all used some psycho-analytic ideas in their efforts to understand the families they worked with and the processes of their work. The English made more use of ideas from learning theory, but the difference was not great. They shared a concern for the suffering of children and a belief that children need families. In spite of some difficulties of vocabulary and definition, they shared a common language for discussing families, children and their work with them. The families described by the social workers also had a lot in common. There were problems of poverty, alcohol abuse, violence, suspected sexual abuse, and problems in relationships between family members. The participants therefore felt that they were dealing with the same problems within a framework of the same understanding of these problems. And yet, as we described in Chapter 1, what actually happened to families and what it meant to be a social worker in the two countries seemed to be very different. Why should this be so?

Focus on the family

In the first place, the French system is primarily concerned with the welfare of children rather than their rights. It is concerned with *éducation* and suffering. It is also grounded in the French Civil Code which sets out both the rights and duties of parents. In the second place, the French see family relationships as having a very powerful reality. The child is a part of his or her family; whatever happens, this fact remains, and the family in this context is not just parents and children. The importance of the family is expressed in the Civil Code which states that parents may not, without grave reason, obstruct contact between grandparents and children. It is also reflected in the injunction that the Children's Judge must always try to gain the agreement of parents to any measures he or she may propose for the child.

It is relatively easy for a French Children's Judge to become involved in the process of a case. The welfare orientation of the system, and the fact that legally admissible evidence of harm is not required, can mean that the judge will be involved in a case at a relatively early stage. The fact that any member of the family can go directly to the judge is another factor which increases the range of situations in which he or she may intervene. However, the cultural importance of 'the family' in France places limitations on the judge's powers. Although a French judge may intervene in situations where their English counterpart could not, once having intervened their powers are far more limited. For example, they are under a statutory obligation to attempt to gain the agreement of parents to any order they may wish to make. This gives parents considerable control over the details of placement; whether the child should be placed in residential care or foster care for example. She or he is also constrained by the power of the social consensus that children should be brought up by, or at the very least, maintain strong links with, their family of origin. Judges therefore sometimes make orders that promote contact between parents and children, and support the rehabilitation of children with their parents in situations where their English counterparts may have given up the struggle.

The judicial role

Once involved, French Children's Judges tend to stay involved, sometimes working with the same family on and off over several years. They review all orders at least every two years. This builds a very different relationship between the judge and the family from anything that currently obtains in England. There are some similarities with pre-Children Act wardship cases, but there are so many other differences in the relationships between the parties concerned, that the comparison is not enlightening. In our French participants' cases, judicial orders came and went in the same family, at times coexisting with administrative orders, at times preceding, and at others, superceding them. It proved impossible to categorise cases in terms of a single type of referral or intervention. In contrast, the English cases shared a common pattern of movement, from preventive work outside the child protection guidelines, to child protection, and thence to legal intervention, to fostering or residential care, to rehabilitation or adoption. Cases could stop at different stages along this continuum, or sometimes avoid the latter stages, but there was a linear progression. The French cases presented a more complex picture, with larger numbers of different types of social workers involved and a broader range of preventive interventions invoked: preventive interventions, administrative orders or judicial orders in no discernable pattern. This was not solely a function of the early and continuing involvement of the judge; it was also a reflection of the efforts made to keep children with their parents or in contact with them.

The French participants often commented on the preoccupation of English social workers with procedure. They noticed it both in terms of the place that procedures took in the discussions of English cases, and the interest of English social workers in the procedures involved in the French cases. It was quite difficult for the English social workers, and researchers, to grasp the apparent absence of formal procedures in French case management, and to believe in the informality of the court system.

The role of the police

An aspect of the English system that the French participants found hard to grasp was the role played by the police. In France, the police have an important but limited role in child protection, and it is one that does not bring them into a working relationship with social workers. If there is an emergency, they are asked to make an investigation by the procurator. They can also be asked to investigate by the Children's Judge if he considers that there is need of evidence of harm, or if there is a possibility of the prosecution of a perpetrator. The role of the English police child protection team, and joint work between the police and social workers, was surprising to the French social workers. One commented that collaboration with the police could be beneficial, but that French social workers would have to change their view of the police if this were to happen.

Social work and the law

The relative ease with which French social workers can invoke the judicial system was demonstrated in the first phase of our research. French and English social workers all studied the same case outline, and gave us their views about what the social worker in the case might have done. The case concerned a family with two children, where, at successive stages, increasing concerns were raised about the well-being of the children, although there was scant evidence of abuse and the parents were unco-operative. The French social workers were considering referral to the judge by the second stage of the case because of the parents' lack of co-operation and the anxieties of the nursery school about the violent behaviour of the 4-year-old child. At this stage, the English social workers felt that there were no legal grounds for inter-vention. At the final stage, the parents were still unco-operative; there were hints of sexual abuse from the 13-year-old and suggestions of violence between the parents as well as a further referral from the nursery school. At this point the English social

workers felt that they could call a case conference; the French
social workers said that they would already have referred the case
to the Children's Judge.

Entering the system

Families in France, as in England, seek help in many different
ways, with varying degrees of enthusiasm or apprehension. Both
French and English participants described families who come of
their own volition to seek help, possibly encouraged by another
professional located elsewhere in the system, as well as families
who were referred by health visitors, schools, nursery schools and
those who were reported by their neighbours. There is however,
one important difference in France and it is that families –
children, parents, uncles, aunts and grandparents – can refer
themselves to the Children's Judge.

Two of the French cases concerned teenage girls whose mothers
asked the judge for help. In both cases this had been suggested by
a professional outside the child protection system. Marie Lecomte
and Sabine Ducroix were both causing their parents concern by
staying out late, running away, missing school and behaving badly.
Mme Lecomte was advised by a social worker attached to her
place of work to go to the local office of the social services
department, where she was seen by Jeanne, an *assistante sociale*.
Jeanne arranged for one of her colleagues, an *éducatrice
spécialisée*, to work with Marie, while she worked with her
mother. Although this all seems recognisable, there are already
differences from the English system. Firstly, it is common in
France for *assistantes sociaux* to work in businesses and factories as
well as in social work agencies, so that there was nothing out of the
way about the origin of this referral. Then, when Mme Lecomte
went to the CISS, she might well have already known who would
be her social worker, because Jeanne was the social worker
attached to her neighbourhood.

The process of case allocation is different in several respects. As
the *assistante sociale du secteur*, Jeanne had a specific population
for whom she was responsible; as we will see later, there are ways
in which the work is shared or passed on, but the initial
responsibility and the initial decision-making rest with an *assistante
sociale du secteur* like Jeanne. The French *assistant social* in the
CISS therefore has a considerable degree of autonomy in deciding
how to react to a referral. Jeanne was able to decide for herself
whether to work with Marie and her mother. She could have been
supported by discussing the case in the *commission d'évaluation*,
where she was a member of multi-disciplinary team which includes

doctors, health visitors and psychologists as well as social workers, but the decision to take the case on was hers, and she decided what resources, in the shape of another worker to work directly with Marie, were needed. The *assistant social du secteur* is held individually responsible for his or her decisions; if, for example, Jeanne failed to report a case of serious child abuse to the Procurator and the child was then killed or seriously injured, she would be liable to prosecution. This does not happen often, but it is a real possibility. It is not surprising that in the first phase of our research, where groups of social workers were discussing a child abuse referral, the *assistante social du secteur* showed far more anxiety than the other French social workers. Cathy, the English participant with whom Jeanne was paired, and who worked in an intake team, felt that she was better supported by the more hierarchical English system.

From the family's point of view the process of getting help was direct and transparent; they knew that they would see the *assistant social* whose patch they lived on, and that initially, this worker would be responsible for decisions about what help was offered to them. They also knew that if they were refused help by Jeanne and wanted to contest this, they could go to the Children's Judge. Indeed, they could have gone straight to the Children's Judge in the first place. This was what Mme Ducroix did, on the advice of a psychologist at the CMPP (child guidance clinic). Sabine and Mme Ducroix were seen by the Children's Judge who made an *ordonance d'observation*, and arranged for Annette, a social worker with the DPJJ, to work with Sabine. Annette worked with Sabine and her mother, with the authority of the judge, and with the responsibility for the decision to work in this way resting with the judge. When Annette was not able to engage effectively with either Sabine or her mother, the judge refused to renew the order, which, as far as Annette's involvement was concerned, meant that the case was closed.

The fact that any child, parent, or closely involved relative can go directly to the Children's Judge creates a situation where families have more choices in the way that they engage with the system and in the way that they define their problems. Dorothée was 14; two years previously she had been placed in residential care on a judicial order following a suicide attempt. Her aunt went to the Children's Judge because she wanted Dorothée to live with her. The judge called a family meeting as a result of which Dorothée went to live with her aunt and an administrative AEMO was made. The point of making an administrative AEMO was that this involved the family in a contract of work with the social worker concerned. As there was no local authority social worker available, the work was done by Joseph, an *éducateur spécialisé* in a voluntary organisation which had a contract to take cases on both administrative and judicial AEMO orders. Dorothée had in the past made allegations of sexual abuse against one of her uncles, which her parents had not believed. She now talked further about the abuse to Joseph, and was able to convince her parents. They decided to prosecute the abuser, who pleaded guilty. If Dorothée's parents had not believed her, and had not decided to prosecute the abuser, Joseph would have gone back to the judge. In this case, because the judge had already been involved, the social worker could go straight to them. In principle, referrals by social workers are made to the Procurator who can, if necessary, take emergency action, but would normally refer the case on to the Children's Judge.

Many of the cases in our study were referred to the participating social workers after the family had been involved with other social workers for some time. This was because a number of the social workers were employed in agencies working as specialist children and family workers, and the initial referral had been to the generic services of the CISS. Our participants had been called on when extra or specialised work was needed. By the time our participants were involved, several other social workers were already on the scene, and continued to be so. The Chapeau family accumulated quite a number of social workers. An *assistante sociale du secteur* worked with the family because they were on her patch; a specialist mental health social worker worked with the father; a *tutrice des allocations familiales* worked with the family on budgeting and financial problems; and our participant, Anne-Marie, supervised the administrative AEMO. The two eldest children, Lucille and Jean, were fostered, and the third child, Jerome, was fostered for part of the week, so there were social workers who were involved with the fostering arrangements and others who worked with the foster parents. The baby, Françoise, was at home, so there was also a health visitor involved. Some of the French participants thought that there were advantages to the English system where there are far fewer different workers involved, and co-ordination is not such a problem; the English participants saw some advantage to having specialist social workers for different aspects of a case, in particular to deal with budgeting and financial problems. One English social worker described the French system as "lavish with social workers", and this reflected a shared perception that the numbers of social workers involved reflected more generous social work resources.

A lot of work had been done with the Chapeau family before there was a judicial intervention, and there were several examples of cases which remained outside the judicial sphere even when there were serious and continuing problems. However, most of the cases demonstrated movement between judicial and administrative interventions. As already described, the Children's Judge who had originally made a placement order for Dorothée Lebrun, brokered an administrative measure after the intervention of Dorothée's aunt. The Chapeau family had, concurrently, a judicial order in relation to their third child and administrative orders in relation to the two older children who were fostered.

One family, which had first been referred to the social services about eight years previously, remained on an administrative order, and was not referred to the Children's Judge, even though the social worker was extremely anxious about the welfare of the children. The Laville family had two daughters aged 14 and 7, and a son of 11. They were first referred to the CISS by the nursery school when the eldest child, Geneviève, was five because of bruising and general neglect. A pattern developed of referral, followed by intervention, followed by improvement which was not sustained for long after the intervention ended. An administrative AEMO was made with the aim of working towards a sustained and sustainable improvement. The measure was accepted by the parents, albeit, somewhat unwillingly. Michelle, their social worker, hoped to continue to work without a judicial order because she felt that a referral to the judge would undermine their trust in her. Nevertheless, she had many concerns about the family, and was not confident that she would be able to continue without a judicial order. We will look again at this case in Chapter 4.

In an emergency, the Procurator can instigate inquiries without referring the case to the Children's Judge, though he has to do so within eight days. The Briquet family was first referred by the psychologist of the CISS to the Procurator because Estelle, the eldest daughter, had indicated in her play and drawings that she might have been sexually abused. The Procurator set up a police investigation, the children were removed from home and there was a medical investigation. Estelle then retracted what she had said, and there was no other evidence of abuse. The children were returned home, and the case was referred to the Children's Judge, who made a judicial AEMO to last for 18 months. This illustrates how in an emergency a case could go to the Children's Judge without prior investigation by the social services department. The children remained at home and Brigitte, our participant, worked

with the parents and the children. The family comprised the
parents and four daughters aged between eight years and a few
months. There had been a boy who had died as a baby two years
previously. The work centred on their grieving for the boy, and
problems over appropriate boundaries in a very chaotic family.
Brigitte also worked with the children, especially the eldest child,
Estelle, trying to gain their confidence. Estelle was the child who
expressed the problems of the family, in school as well as at home.
The question of the reality or otherwise of the alleged sexual abuse
was not central to the work with the parents or the children.
During the research period, the AEMO was due to end, but at
Brigitte's request the judge made a further order for a year. The
order was made in spite of the fact that the parents were
co-operating with Brigitte, and the children could not be said to be
in danger. Brigitte felt the order made the parents face the fact
that there were still problems in the functioning of the family and
that there was still work to do. M. Briquet was not pleased with
the continuation of the order, and the judge had to exert his
authority to bring home to the parents the seriousness of the
situation. The English participant was struck by the fact that it was
possible, under these circumstances, for a judicial order to be
made. This family faced a further tragedy, as, not long after the
second order was made, their youngest daughter died suddenly of
hepatitis, and thereafter their mourning for this second loss
dominated the work.

The examples of the Laville, Briquet and Chapeau families all
demonstrate long term work with very precarious families, where
the parents had poor parenting skills and psychiatric problems; in
each case there was violence or alcohol abuse. Not all the children
were still living at home, but for all of them some form of AEMO
was in place, and the aim was to maintain strong family ties, even
when they were fostered.

Conclusion

In this chapter we have described how the French system engages
with families and how the children are protected. This is based on
the cases of the French social workers who participated in our
research. They demonstrate how the French and the English child
protection systems generate very different experiences for both
social workers and families. A central difference is the relationship
between the families, the social workers and the law. This is
expressed in France by the greater readiness of families and social
workers to use the law, whereas in England the law is, and is
supposed to be, a last resort.

French social work tends to be consensual and flexible, but with considerable potential for overlap and confusion. English social work, by contrast, tends to be hierarchical and highly organised.

Underpinning these differences are markedly different structures of law, state benefits and welfare services which radically affect the needs of clients and the roles played by their social workers.

The complex web of French social work is brought together at two points, where decision making is vested in a single person. One of these is the Children's Judge, and the other, in the administrative sphere, is the ASE *Inspecteur*. Both the judge and the *Inspecteur* observe the consensual approach to work with families but nevertheless have the power and the duty to make decisions, if necessary against that consensus.

Chapter 4:
Keeping the Family Together

This chapter considers preventive work undertaken by French social workers with families in which there are concerns about the abuse or neglect of their children. At the outset we ask: what and who is perceived to be a problem? That is, who are the candidates for French child protection social work interventions and why are they perceived as problematic? We go on to ask about the aims of these interventions and the 'solutions', they offer.

Problems and solutions

On the face of it, French social workers identify and deal with the same catalogue of family problems as English workers. However, ideas about the impact and meaning of these problems are rather different. Though the social work assessment may point to family breakdown or threats to the child's safety, interventions tend to aim at the reintegration of the family and the restoration of a family life which is conducive to the proper care and upbringing of children. Thus the problems posed by immature parents, neglectful mothers, alcoholic fathers, abusing uncles and so on, are more likely to be seen as an indication that families need support, advice and guidance, than as a sign of parental failure and familial disintegration. They are seldom taken as sufficient reason to remove the child permanently from the natural family. Social work interventions are therefore designed both to keep the family together and enable it to undertake its proper social role in the *éducation* of the child: its development, in the broadest sense.

These twin aspirations may be said to underpin French social work interventions in the field of child protection. French social workers describe their work as aiming to "help the family to sort out its problems", "to improve the family climate", "to lead the parents to a better understanding of their involvement and responsibilities in the *éducation* of their children" and "to encourage the family to become more closely-knit [*soudé*], in spite of conflicts." Although a child may be deemed to be at risk of neglect or maltreatment, its permanent or long-term removal from the family, according to one French worker, would merely absolve parents of their responsibilities and serve as an encouragement to some to relinquish them altogether. Rather, he suggests, they need reminding of their obligations and help in fulfilling them.

The ethical onus on French social workers to keep families together makes the ways in which they attempt to 'protect' children noticeably different. In Chapter 5 we shall see how the French legal system underpins this orientation. In this chapter we look at how the actions and decisions of social workers in France are affected. Some of the more obvious differences lie in the relationships between social workers and families, their methods of working and, as we have seen in Chapter 2, in the availability of material and non-material resources to support these. The most significant difference, which will be considered in Chapter 6, concerns the removal of children from the natural family.

Building trust

The emphasis on keeping families together makes it more likely that French social workers and families will have a positive relationship. Several factors contribute to this relationship of trust. Firstly, the likelihood, and legal possibility, of the family being split up permanently are very low and virtually impossible without parents' permission; this means that, on the whole, social work intervention involves working with the child in the family. Removing the child, as will be seen later, is viewed as a temporary step to assist the reunification of the family, not as a stage in its separation from the family. Secondly, the family's co-operation and agreement is necessary for administrative measures to be instituted. Thirdly, unlike their English counterparts, French social workers in this field do not need to search for evidence of child maltreatment in order to work with a family. Parents are therefore less likely to see them as acting against their interests. This, together with the proactive nature of their interventions, means that the involvement of social workers in family problems is potentially less threatening for French parents and their children. If, on the other hand, parents know that the presentation of evidence against them is a legal keystone in the protection of their children and believe that the social worker is engaged in the collection of such evidence, it is not surprising that the climate can be one of mistrust. In such situations, it is predictably difficult for families and social workers to feel that they are working in 'partnership' with one another.

An English case served to highlight this difference for an English social worker and her French opposite number. Both remarked on the less antagonistic relationships which seem to exist between social workers and parents in France. In the case of 12-year-old Sally, social workers were concerned that her mother's severe alcohol problems were hindering Sally's emotional and educational development. When, after she had refused permission for Sally to be placed in a foster home, the mother discovered that the social worker, with Sally's agreement, had sought and obtained an Interim Care Order without her knowledge and involvement, she was not only angry with the social services department but continued to be hostile and unco-operative throughout the research period. Catherine, a psychologist with an ASE family placements team, felt that a different kind of social work intervention was needed; one which focused on the mother's problems as well and placed a premium on partnership. The importance placed on the co-operation of families was shared by other French social workers, who saw it as typical of social worker-family relations in their experience.

Taking risks

This emphasis on working with families appeared to be driven by professional as well as legal imperatives. Several of the French social workers described the priority that they placed on building-up a relationship of trust with the family, even if this meant knowingly taking risks. Maintaining a "precarious balance" between the risks of destroying this trust if the police and judiciary were called in, when sexual abuse was suspected, and the risk to the child of such abuse, was seen to be necessary by these workers, if their interventions were to make a long term difference to the functioning of the family. Without a relationship of trust, the necessary work of assisting parents to recognise and exercise their responsibilities could not take place effectively.

What did this mean in practice? What kind of risks were being taken when social workers placed primary importance on establishing a climate of trust with families? In the case of Brigitte, an *éducatrice*, the children concerned had given the CISS psychologist the impression, through their drawings and discussion, that sexual abuse was taking place at home. Although a police investigation revealed nothing, the suspicions of abuse continued. Brigitte, rather than pursuing these suspicions, decided to "remain neutral" regarding the allegations and to work instead with the family by helping them to introduce "boundaries" into their everyday interactions. Although one of her objectives was to work with them on the issue of sexuality, it was thought that this would be made more possible if she built up a relationship of trust first.

Michelle, another *éducatrice*, also described the need, as she saw it, to engage the family as a whole in order to develop her work with them, rather than initiating an investigation which she saw as hindering this possibility. In spite of revelations of sexual abuse by the oldest child, aged 13, Michelle's first aim was to reduce the child's feelings of guilt and responsibility rather than search for more evidence. She was aware of the risks she was taking, and did not take them lightly but, in her view, the need to build up trust meant that things should not be done too quickly. Furthermore, she feared that bringing the case into the judicial domain would not help the family to sort out its problems.

Several differences emerge here between English and French attitudes and practices in this critical area of social work. The identification of risk in general seems as acute in France as it is in England but the responses to that risk, and interpretations of it, are as we have seen, somewhat different. Although French workers would seem to be no more willing than English ones to leave a child in a dangerous situation, their perceptions of what constitutes danger are different. This applies particularly to sexual abuse. Furthermore, their definitions of risk extend to dangers to the family as well as the child. This means that although social workers on either side of the channel have 'bottom lines' of acceptability, they are drawn differently. For example, French social workers define sexual abuse similarly to their English counterparts but view the risks differently. They appear to have a more elastic approach which allows them to respond with less urgency, because the unacceptable behaviour is not itself defined as the 'crisis'. They are therefore able to engage in planned, proactive work rather than making an instant reaction.

Team work

What kind of resources are available on the other side of the channel to make this kind of risk-taking possible? According to both French and English social workers, a key factor in the management of such high risk situations is team work and the shared decision-making and mutual support which this makes possible. Although several English social workers were surprised at the lack of regular supervision that their French colleagues received, the latter pointed out that the joint decision-making at the core of the team approach made supervision less necessary for them than for workers bearing individual responsibility for cases. Furthermore, as several English participants enviously noted, there was much easier access to psychological resources, in the form of a team psychologist, who could be routinely drawn on by the French social workers, not only for assistance in work with clients but also as a source of information and support for themselves.

Working as a team appears to promote a sense of solidarity that makes each team member feel more secure and more able to work with flexibility. Shared decision-making spreads both responsibility and accountability; this in turn provides an opportunity to be more imaginative as well as more elastic in planning possible courses of action. An additional and very important feature of this shared decision-making, especially from the point of view of social worker accountability, is the position and role that the Children's Judge plays in the process. As we saw earlier, the fact that the judge has ultimate responsibility for decision-making means that French social workers can be more creative in their work than their English counterparts. In addition, the built-in approach-ability of the judge means that, as one French worker noted, the *audience* provides real opportunities to make suggestions about future courses of action.

Multi-disciplinary teams

A further feature of this division of labour and responsibility in France is the multi-disciplinary team. The *équipe pluridisciplinaire* includes professionals from health, social work and legal agencies whose involvement and responsibilities in the case are co-ordinated by the Children's Judge. Although there can also be communication breakdowns in this system, it is probably easier for French practitioners to undertake high risk work with families. French social workers, unlike their English counterparts, are not hamstrung by having to bear the lion's share of responsibility for a case without power to act in ways which their professional judgement might suggest. They know that if, in a high risk situation, they need to act, the legal and administrative means to do so will be immediately available to them. It appears that the powers and responsibilities of the professionals involved in child protection are relatively well balanced. Clearly this has significant implications for the ways in which social workers do their job but also for how they feel about their work and their ability to make an impact upon the situation in which they are required to intervene.

Working with the family

How do French social workers do their job? How is the ethos of keeping the family together reflected in their work? How does the flexibility that we have talked about translate into social work practice with children and families on the other side of the channel?

The French social workers described practice methodologies which, though diverse, focused primarily on changing family relationships. Some workers were keen to distinguish between in-depth work, which focused on the 'real' or 'underlying' problems of intra-familial dynamics and the emotional aspects of family relationships, and more concrete work, which was seen as addressing the everyday 'symptoms' of these problems. While this was often the starting point of the intervention, its purpose was to begin the process of building a relationship of trust between family and social worker. This engagement was perceived as securing the ground and laying the foundations for the more difficult, but essential, in-depth work needed to enable the family to change in the long term.

In the case of 15-year-old Sabine, who was referred by the CMPP psychologist, her poor school attendance, scholastic difficulties and frequent absences from home were seen as symptoms of the underlying emotional problems between Sabine and her mother. The mother's constant ambivalence towards professional interventions, on the part of psychologists and the *éducatrice*, suggested to the team that a further problem of 'denial' needed to be worked on. However, rather than tackling this head-on, it was decided to establish a 'climate of confidence' with the family first. To this end, when Mme Ducroix requested that Sabine's educational problems be prioritised the team went along with this, hoping to get round gradually to the more complex problems that they felt neither mother nor daughter were facing up to. A programme was developed to support Sabine educationally, which involved a calendar of meetings and educational assessments, and the order made by the Children's Judge, was confined to the educational aspects of the problem.

Although this more concrete work serves to engage families, it is not seen only as a means to this end; it also begins the work of improving family relationships. However, the strategies for doing this surprised and interested the English social workers for the process of initiating change focused on *actions éducatives*, working with family members in and through the activities of everyday life, in the family home. Our participants described helping with care, playing with the children, drawing, having lunch with the family, working on hygiene problems by helping to clean the home. Taking the children away on outings, weekend 'mini-camps' and summer camps enabled *éducateurs* and other team members to work with the children in a different social milieu. In both settings these interventions tended to be essentially practical, in the sense that they were activity-based, but the problems that they sought to address were not the manifest behaviours but the underlying tensions in family relations of which they were seen to be symptomatic. This approach contrasts with the behavioural approaches, which are more familiar on this side of the Channel. These emphasise the management of problematic behaviour in order to minimise family disruption rather than a quest for the meaning of that behaviour.

The work of Michelle, an *éducatrice* with a voluntary agency, whose calculated risk-taking was discussed earlier, illustrates the scope of this work. Her aim was to work with the family's 'dysfunctional communication' by tackling it on a number of different levels, using a variety of methods. This complex mixture was guided by a strategy based on a psychological analysis which drew on psychoanalytic and systems theory. She saw the different concrete elements – dirty children, school absenteeism, educational difficulties – as tangible problems that she could work with by providing educational support and by helping to clean the home. However, she also viewed them as manifestations of the 'deeper' problems of this dysfunctional family. The suspected child sexual abuse was also viewed as being both a problem in its own right and as symptomatic of the family's confused communication. She used her participation in bedroom cleaning with the children to signal the problem of 'boundaries' and to propose that the youngest child be moved out of the parental bedroom. The children were taken on a three day mini-camp organised by the team in order to engage them and to observe the sibling relationships and the children's relationships with others. At the same time, Michelle's aim was to work with the parents on their underlying communication problems by talking with them about the difficulties within their relationship and with their children (She knew that they were hitting them.) Her aim in doing this was to assist them to recognise these difficulties and to develop 'a capacity for change'.

On the whole, the French social workers used a similarly wide range of proactive interventions which were designed to help the family change. The methods used depended, to a large extent, on the kind of practitioner concerned and their professional brief. For example, *éducateurs* and *assistantes sociales* have different remits such that the latter are generally more involved in arranging access to welfare and practical assistance whereas, as we have seen, *éducateurs* work at the psychological level. However, within these broad differences there is room for manoeuvre. The particular approach that workers use may be guided by their view of the role and their motivation to pursue certain aspects of it. Psychoanalytic perspectives tend to provide the bases of intervention strategies but the weight given to these and the ways in which they are translated into practice vary from worker to worker. One *éducatrice*, for example, favoured an explicitly psychoanalytic approach that involved prioritising her interpretations, both of the family's behaviour and her own responses to it and which concentrated, in practice, on the development of insight by talking and discussion.

Although these French social workers used psychological analyses to underpin their work and perceived themselves as being capable of bringing about change in the emotional and psychological functioning of the family, they did not see themselves as 'therapists' or as being engaged in 'therapeutic work' in the way that English social workers understand the term. Perhaps this was because of their ease of access to professional psychological resources. The formal division of labour in this respect meant that not only did they not see the psychological or therapeutic role as theirs but also that they could expect, in practice, that this work would be done by the team psychologist or referred to specialised psychological services.

This contrasted with the experience of English social workers, who saw therapeutic work, especially in-depth, individual work with children, as a key feature of their interventions. Ironically, both they and their French colleagues saw this as a role which English social workers could not fulfill because of pressure to 'process' cases. Perhaps this pressure and the accompanying requirement to follow procedures has contributed to an emphasis on easily implemented solutions to here-and-now problems. Task-centred work, based on behavioural approaches, has found increasing favour amongst hard pressed English social workers and their managers, not necessarily as a reflection of an ideological espousal of behaviourism but because it fits the bill in these respects. In French eyes this focus risked ignoring the deep-seated emotional problems of family relationships which they saw as the 'real' cause of their clients' difficulties. However, in spite of these reservations, which English social workers to some extent share, we found that these approaches were of some interest to French social workers.

The role of the psychologist

Most of the French families received some attention from a psychologist for the purposes of assessment or 'treatment', from a variety of sources. Psychologists are employed in most social welfare and health agencies and families could expect to come in contact with them through CISS, ASE, CMPP or PMI as well as voluntary agencies. As we have seen, their approach is mainly psychodynamic, focusing on family relationships but they also draw on systems theory. Predictably perhaps, behavioural psychology, stemming from the Anglo-American tradition of learning theory, is of less interest to French psychologists. Its emphasis on solving problems by changing behaviour was thought to be too superficial to be useful in changing family relationships. Psychological assistance could come in the form of direct contact, in face-to-face meetings, or indirectly through the contribution of the psychologist in team case discussions.

Conclusion

In this chapter we have seen how French social workers' involvement with parents and children is based on a set of ideas about the social importance of the family. The cultural ideal of the integrated family guides expectations of what is both desirable and achievable and underpins the provision of resources and practice methodologies. Space is given to risk-taking and proactive work that is intended to bring about positive change in family functioning. This demonstrates an optimism that is less noticeable on this side of the Channel. What it is like to be on the 'receiving end' of these sorts of interventions is hard to assess, though emphases on the voluntary agreement of parents and on winning the trust of families suggest that alienation and antagonism are less likely.

The clear and formalised division of labour, which has important repercussions for client access to resources, also has major implications for social workers' experience of their own abilities to make a positive difference to the lives of their clients. It is apparent from the French cases that the division of labour was matched by the provision of resources which enabled this separation of roles to be effective. In addition, the existence of other professionals in the multi-disciplinary and agency teams meant that French social workers could share the responsibility of decision-making and could afford to be adventurous, with the sanction of others. This in turn meant that they were less likely to feel under pressure to make the 'right' decision, more likely to feel secure about their purpose and confident about their abilities to fulfill it. Nevertheless, French social workers, like their English counterparts, do have to make difficult decisions about whether, and for how long, children should be separated from their families. In Chapters 5 and 6 we consider the ways in which the child's removal from the natural family comes about.

Chapter 5: Placing Children Outside the Family I: The Judge and the Inspecteur

In the last chapter we considered the work undertaken with families whose children, or some of them, remained in the family. This chapter deals with those children who were placed outside their families. In France, placement outside the family can take place without a judicial order, if the parents are in agreement and want the placement. However, the Children's Judge is involved in some way with all children who live in residential or foster care.

The process of placing children can only be understood in terms of the relationshp between the judge, the family and the social worker, and between the social worker, the family and the multi-disciplinary team of the CISS.

The relationships between the judge and the family, and the judge and the social worker, are different from anything which exists in the English system. This difference is evident from the atmosphere of the judge's *audience* with the family.

The judge

A member of the research team sat in on a French judge's morning *audience*. The difference from a morning spent in an English family proceedings court could hardly have been more striking. The courtroom was, in fact, the judge's office, a spacious room, large enough to hold two desks and some filing cabinets. There were also about a dozen upright chairs, a number of them placed in a row in front of the judge's desk. A room led off this office, where the judge's clerk worked. Outside the judge's office there was a large hallway used as a waiting room, with chairs and some toys, and a door leading into the clerk's office. We were initially taken into the clerk's office and introduced to her. While we were waiting for the morning's proceedings to begin, a young woman in her late twenties came into the room. This was the judge. We were given seats to one side of her office, and she then went to the waiting room herself to call in the family and their social worker. The family, a man and woman with two sons in their late teens, and the social worker, sat side by side facing the judge across her desk. The room was formal, but no more so than a bank or a clinic. The *audience* lasted for about half an hour. The first family was accustomed to meeting the judge. The two boys were the youngest of a large family, and were subject to something similar to a supervision order designed to promote training and job finding. The social worker reported that little progress had been made with the older boy, who was not taking advantage of available opportunities. The younger boy was more responsive and had special needs because of a growth problem. The parents were passive, saying that they had been doing their best. The judge spoke to the two boys, telling the oldest, who was 17, that there was no point making an order aimed at helping him to find work because he was not co-operating and the resources could be better used on someone else. The younger boy was given a further order, and agreed to work with the social worker. The parents were told very firmly that they should support the work being done by the social worker. The judge was authoritative, very clear in her communications with the family and very direct; the family, both parents and children, appeared to be well able to say what they wanted to her, although they showed respect for her. At the end of the *audience*, the mother said that she wanted to speak to the judge alone. The judge sent out the rest of the family and the social worker. The mother then told the judge that she was worried about one of her grandchildren; her son and his girlfriend had a young child, and she thought that the child was not being properly cared for. She had seen bruises, she said, and her son and his girlfriend drank too much. The judge suggested that she should go to the social services. The mother said that she had done this, and also made an anonymous complaint by telephone, but that social services had done nothing. The judge then explained that she could only act if the mother would write down what she was now saying. She encouraged the mother to write something down and give it to the clerk there and then. The mother agreed to do this and left with the intention of taking action. The mother, who was poor with a long experience of family problems, seemed to be able to speak to the judge, who was half her age, with respect and confidence.

There was uncertainty about whether the second family to be seen that day would actually turn up because they had failed to come to a previous *audience*. They had been sent the notice of the *audience* on the first occasion by post; this time, the letter had been delivered by the police. The family comprised the parents and five children aged between five and twelve. The four oldest children accompanied their parents to the *audience*. The family had been referred eight months earlier because the children were out of control. They had been seen by a judge who made an order for an investigation, to be carried out by a social worker from the COAE, the Ministry of Justice social work team. Once again, the judge fetched the family from the waiting area, and family and social worker sat facing her. The judge asked the parents about their failure to attend the previous audience. She did not accept their excuses. She sent the children to the waiting area in order to discuss the problem with the parents and the social worker. She said that the parents had failed to protect the children from anxiety about their own problems, and to provide security for them. The judge described the children as "sad". The father was employed, and they were owner-occupiers, but he was alcoholic and they faced possible eviction in two months' time. The social worker said she thought the mother was depressed, but it was not clear whether this was a psychiatric diagnosis or the social worker's opinion. The parents did not feel that there were problems about controlling the children, but accepted that they were not protecting them from anxiety. The father said that he was controlling his drinking, and the mother agreed, albeit, somewhat reluctantly. The judge decided to make an AEMO order for one year and warned the parents that if they were evicted, she would be likely to make a placement order for the children. She then sent the parents out and called the children back in. She explained the situation to them, and made it clear that their anxieties had been acknowledged by her.

The third *audience* illustrated the possibilities for confusion in the French system. A voluntary organisation held an administrative AEMO on three children living with their mother who had an alcohol problem. One of the children, a nine-year-old, had been referred to the judge by his school because he had hit a dinner lady. A brief investigation by a SEAT social worker failed to reveal that an administrative AEMO was held by the voluntary organisation. The *saissin* was therefore only made for the nine-year-old child. The voluntary organisation holding the AEMO was about to refer all three children to the Children's Judge because of anxieties about the children, the mother's drinking and her violent and alcoholic cohabitee. The flat was in her name, but he visited frequently and was violent towards her and the children. As the *saissin* had only been made for one of the children, the judge was unable to make an order for all three. She decided to postpone making an order for three weeks at which time she arranged an *audience* for the whole family. The judge discussed the situation with the social worker before the family came in. She then asked the mother and child to come in and explained why she was not able to make an order immediately. She said she planned to have a further *audience* in three weeks; at which time she said she would make an order and, if there had been no signs of progress, it would be a placement order, not an AEMO. She explained to the mother that it was her duty to protect the children from the violence of her cohabitee.

In all these cases, the judge spoke at some length, setting out the position. When she moved from this to a dialogue with the families, they responded well, entering the discussion and maintaining their own point of view. Although the children played a relatively small part in the proceedings, they did have a chance to be heard. They also had full and clear explanations about what was going to happen and why. The social workers took a low profile in the court hearings. The main dialogue was between the judge and the family, although the social workers were consistently brought into the discussion by the judge. This contrasts with the English system, where the social worker often plays the major role in court, but can also be virtually excluded. Brigitte, a French social worker, was taken to a High Court hearing by her English pair, Carol. Brigitte was surprised by the level of anxiety Carol felt and the time she spent preparing the case. She was taken aback when neither Carol nor the parents were called into court. The lawyers were the only people seen by the judge.

French social workers are in frequent contact with the judge about cases where an order exists, particularly where a child is still living at home. Even when the child is in a placement, there may be continuing telephone or personal contact with the judge. French social workers sometimes go to see the judge in circumstances in which their English counterparts might approach their team leader or child protection specialist. For example, a 14-year-old girl on an AEMO order turned up at about six o'clock one evening at a voluntary agency's office. She had had a row with her parents and did not want to go home because she was afraid her father would beat her. She wanted somewhere to go for the night.

The social worker had to telephone the judge for his decision about whether she could be accommodated in a residential establishment. The social workers do not always agree with the judge's decisions, and have their own views about what should happen, but they have to accept the authority of the judge.

When referring a case to, making an assessment for, or reporting to the judge when a case is reviewed, the social worker must write a report. These reports are not normally seen by parents. They are shorter than court reports written by English social workers or Guardians ad Litem, and less formal than reports to child protection case conferences. These reports are not concerned primarily with the question of who did what. Rather, they consider the nature and quality of the relationships between the family members, their relationship with the social worker, the potential for change in the situation and the social worker's plans for bringing about such change. In this report the judge requires the social worker to make a clear recommendation for future intervention if this is deemed appropriate. In a review report, the judge requires a statement concerning the extent to which the aims of an order have been achieved. These reports are written with the expectation that the judge will be familiar with the language of social work rather than simply the language of the law. There is normally, though not, of course, on all occasions, a mutual respect between the judge and the social worker, each valuing the other's professional skills and knowledge.

The Inspecteur

The role of the ASE *Inspecteur* in the administrative sphere is similar to that of the Children's Judge in the legal sphere. There are normally four *Inspecteurs* in each DISS and they are the decision makers in this specialist children's service. They control resources and are the ultimate authority in the administrative sphere of the French child protection system.

The *Inspecteur* has a wide range of functions in respect of children who are referred to the specialist children and families service (Thévenet 1990). She or he is not a social worker, although some social workers take up these posts. It is more usual for an *Inspecteur* to have a legal or administrative background. The *Inspecteur* sanctions all administrative orders and all referrals, via the Procurator, to the Children's Judge. As we have noted, in the case of administrative AEMOs or placements, the *Inspecteur* is required to gain the agreement of the family to the decision. Prior to this the *Inspecteur* must also gain the agreement of the CISS multi-disciplinary team to the plan to be negotiated with the parents. He or she also has responsibility for the residential and foster care resources administered by the ASE and decisions made about the children placed in them. Ruth, who was paired with Marie-Claire, an *Inspecteur*, I was struck by the extensive responsibilities of this role and by Marie-Clarie's relative youth and lack of anxiety. Ruth described an interview between Marie-Claire and a teenager placed in one of the ASE residential establishments. This young person was in trouble with the managers of the home, and was taken to task by Marie-Claire with a directness which Ruth found startling. Marie-Claire's view of her responsibilities was that she knew and understood the laws and regulations, and that she had therefore no particular reason to be anxious.

Before a decision about the placement of children reaches the ASE *Inspecteur* or the Children's Judge, it is normally considered by the multi-disciplinary team of the CISS. The support of this team is considered very important by the social workers employed in the CISS. It is also important to the social workers in other agencies, who may be working on a case with a judicial order, that they involve this team in decisions regarding placement. Negotiations over the placement of a child may therefore involve meetings with a large number of people. The parents of the child are not usually included in these meetings, but by dint of the principle that placements are subject to negotiation with parents, they still retain some power in the situation. Where there is no judicial order, and the placement is made at the parents' request, they are able to decide between a residential placement or a foster placement. The social worker might disagree with the parents over this, but the parents' power to choose is real. The *Inspecteur* meets the parents to agree upon the service to be provided, and what will be expected of parents and children. Where the placement is made by order of the judge, the parents still have some power to choose. The judge has to seek the agreement of the parents to his or her plan, and parents can appeal against his or her decision. Where the child will be placed is, therefore, usually negotiated between the judge and the parents. Although the local authority provides the residential establishment or fostering placement, it takes no part in the placement decision. As noted in Chapter 2, residential care is often viewed positively in France by both parents and workers, and this affects the decision made.

A child in foster care or a residential placement continues to be regarded as part of her family. This is supposedly so in England just as much as France, and yet there appeared to be considerable differences between the two countries in the way that a placement away from home was viewed by children, parents and workers. To summarise, in France, rehabilitation remained a central goal and a real possibility. By contrast, it appeared that in the English cases the goal of rehabilitation was abandoned relatively early on and alternative goals, concerned with long term placement away from home, became paramount.

Several of the French cases involved children who were placed in foster care or residential establishments. In the Ivoire family, there were four children, aged 11, 8, 6 and 5. Madame Ivoire had an alcohol problem, there was conflict in the family and they were in debt. They were referred to the judge by the *assistant social* of the CISS. In the first place an OMO was made for three months, and then an AEMO. After several months, the parents agreed to a voluntary placement for the three younger children, while the eldest child went to live with his maternal grandparents. The social worker from JCLT, the *assistant social* and the workers in the residential home liaised with each other. Some months later, there was no change in the parents' behaviour, and they were visiting their children less frequently. The judge then made a placement order for one year for the three younger children and a further AEMO for the eldest child who remained with his grandmother. Rehabilitation of the younger children still remained the aim.

The Bourdon family had been involved with social workers for several years. Their four sons were 19, 16, 15 and 11. In 1989 the family had been joined by M. Jourdain, a friend of M. Bourdon. The two middle boys disclosed that M. Jourdain had been sexually abusing them; he admitted this and was sentenced to two years in prison and to a three year suspended sentence. In the same year, Mme. Bourdon left home with her boyfriend. The oldest son was living with his maternal grandmother, but the younger three remained at home with their father, who drank and was violent. In 1991, the 15-year-old boy was referred to the judge by the school because he was truanting. The judge made a *mesure de liberté surveillée* on the three older children and, shortly after, an AEMO in respect of Jonathon, the youngest. By this time M. Jourdain had come out of prison and was back in the neighbourhood. Joseph, the *éducateur* who was employed by the voluntary agency, working with Jonathon, became anxious about the possibility of further sexual abuse by M. Jourdain who was visiting the family. Joseph asked for a review by the judge, and there was an *audience* attended by both the parents, the children and the social workers. The work with the older boys was being undertaken by SEAT. It was decided to place all the children on another AEMO for two months in order that Joseph could continue to work with Jonathon. The judge decided, without much concrete evidence, that abuse was taking place. There was then some difficulty in finding a suitable residential placement for Jonathon, and in the meanwhile he remained at home. Vickie, who was paired with Joseph, commented on the fact that Jonathon was allowed to remain at home, and that although Joseph was making every effort to find a placement, he was not anxious that if anything happened to Jonathon he would himself be blamed. She felt that in a similar situation she would have been acutely anxious, and that her department would not have been able to risk a child remaining at home once an order had been made.

In the Chapeau family, introduced in Chapter 3, the children, Lucille and Jean, were fostered, and had not been cared for by their parents for some years. They were now six and four, and had recently been placed, together, with the same carers. Anne-Marie, the *éducatrice*, was involved with the whole family, but was working with Lucille and Jean towards their rehabilitation with their parents. Anne-Marie doubted that this could be achieved, and thought that open adoption might offer the best solution. However, the way the case was discussed made it clear that the children were still considered to be an essential part of the family.

The greatest divergence between France and England, with regard to placement, concerns the treatment of younger children. Mention has already been made of the two eldest children in the Chapeau family, who seemed likely to remain in their foster placement for some time to come, while attempts continued to enable their return home. One of the English cases, by contrast, demonstrated a speed of movement towards adoption that the French social workers found breathtaking. Ms. Hall was a single parent with three children. She was a drug user, and had some involvement in criminal activities. Some time previously she had become depressed and unable to manage, and her children had been taken into care. (This was before the implementation of the Children Act.) After some months, the elder children were returned to her care, but Richard, the youngest, who was then two, remained in foster care. At the beginning of the research, Ms. Hall was expecting another child in a few months, and the local authority had decided that she would be unable to cope with Richard's return, and that he should therefore be adopted. By the end of the research, Richard had been placed for adoption, against his mother's wishes. Marie-Claire found this very hard to understand. She could not see why this one child should have been kept in care when the others were returned, and she found it very surprising that it was possible for adoption to be planned without the mother's consent. This case has many points of similarity with that of André Fargeau discussed in the next chapter.

Another case concerning a four-year-old in foster care showed a similar approach on the part of the Children's Judge. Sophie Gilet was placed in a *pouponnière* at the age of four months after her twin sister died and her mother was unable to manage. Mme. Gilet kept up regular contact for about a year, but then her visits ceased. The case was referred to the judge by the *pouponnière*. The judge made a placement order, warning Mme. Gilet that Sophie could be declared abandoned if she did not visit her. There were regular visits when the judge demanded, followed by protracted absences. Finally the *Inspecteur* had a meeting with Mme. Gilet at which she was asked for her consent to Sophie's adoption. After this, Mme. Gilet began to visit Sophie regularly and a rehabilitation plan was devised. At the time the research ended, Sophie had progressed from day visits, through overnight stays, to spending whole weekends with her mother. The plan was that she should soon return home with a judicial AEMO to support the return.

This case demonstrates the power of the judge in promoting rehabilitation, even in opposition to the *Inspecteur*.

Apart from these two cases, adoption was only mentioned in one other French case. Anne-Marie raised the question whether it would be better for Lucille and Jean Chapeau, who looked like remaining in long term foster care, to be adopted. The form of adoption that she considered was *adoption simple*; which can only take place at the request of the birth parents, and involves maintaining some links with the birth family. It can also be revoked at the request of the birth parents, if the child is still a minor, and of the adopters, if the child is over 15 (Verdier 1988). Full adoption, *adoption plénière*, which would have been the form of adoption contemplated for André and Sophie, includes a complete break between the child and her family of origin in the way that used to be the norm in England. *Adoption simple* could be used like open adoption, but this does not seem to happen in France and *adoption simple* was not regarded by the French social workers as a usual part of the range of placement possibilities for a child.

The differences in the attitude to adoption between the social workers of England and France will be explored in later chapters.

Conclusion

While social workers in both countries face similar problems of shortages of suitable placements, the French social workers are under less pressure to place children quickly. In both countries, the parents had some control over where children were placed when the case was in the administrative sphere. However, in both countries, parental agreement to an administrative decision could be influenced by a fear of legal intervention if agreement was withheld. The placement recommendations of French CISS social workers had to be discussed in the multi-disciplinary team, or between CISS and the voluntary agency involved in the case, before it could be sanctioned by the *Inspecteur*. The CISS team therefore had a great deal of influence on the placements offered to families. The *Inspecteur* then had to negotiate with the parents about the placement and on the contact between child and family.

Once families entered the legal sphere the differences were greater. French judges must try to gain the agreement of parents because the expectation of all parties is that the placement will lead to rehabilitation. Parents also know that, save for exceptional circumstances, their children cannot be adopted without their agreement. The decision to place a child in residential or foster care is normally negotiated between the parents and the judge, but the judge is responsible, and has the final word. She or he also has to be consulted about the actual placement chosen. The maximum length of an order is two years, but the judge reviews the placement more frequently, and a child's placement cannot be changed without the judge's agreement.

French parents retain more power in the situation than their English counterparts, even though their power is circumscribed. The power to decide the nature of the child's placement in France lies either between the parents and the ASE *Inspecteur*, in the administrative sphere, or between the parents and the Children's Judge, in the legal sphere. It does not, as it does in England, lie with the social worker.

Adoption assumes a very different role in France and is rarely considered as an option for the future of a child who is the responsibility of the local authority. It is likely that this apparent lack of interest in adoption in France is linked to the emphasis on rehabilitation and the maintenance of the child within its family of origin.

Chapter 6: Placing Children Outside the Family II: the Practice of Social Work

The very different conceptions, in France and England, of what are desirable, legitimate and possible solutions for mistreated children are clearly demonstrated in the area of alternative care. This chapter looks at decisions made in France about whether, when and for how long children should be removed from their families. As in England, there are three main alternatives to remaining at home: adoption, foster care and residential care. However, the purpose, frequency and likelihood of these alternatives being taken up is very different in France.

From this side of the Channel perhaps the most noticeable manifestation of the twin emphases on keeping families together and assisting them to function more effectively, is a widespread reluctance to remove children permanently from the family home. Separating children from their natural parents is thought of as both socially undesirable and inimical to the development of the child. Permanent removal is regarded as a measure of last resort. Temporary removal is used more frequently but as a stage in the process of reuniting the family, rather than as a stage in its ultimate separation. This means that adoption and long-term placement in residential or foster care are, in theory at least, unlikely to happen. However, it is possible for a child to remain in residential or foster care for some years in spite of the stated aim to restore it to the natural family.

Adoption

As we have noted, adoption is much less widespread in France than it is in England; the child is much more likely to go into residential or foster care if the family situation is considered to be problematic. If this is the case, when is adoption likely to occur? It is very rare for older children to be adopted; the most frequent candidates for adoption are babies, whose parents have given their consent, or those who have been legally declared 'abandoned'. Given the French valorisation of the family it is not surprising that the law does not favour adoption and that the 'authorities' there wait longer than their English counterparts before actively considering it. In French eyes families need to be given every chance to become functional and any small gesture is taken as a sign of improvement. In English eyes this strategy, which appears to involve a greater tolerance of parental neglect or lack of interest, is often seen to work against the interests of the child. From this perspective, children are not only exposed to unnecessary risks in the present; their opportunities for future security are also compromised. The case of the Fargeau children illustrates these contrasting perspectives.

The case of André came to light in a *Commission de Prevention* when he was five months old. He had been hospitalised since birth because of cardiac and other problems but had only been visited once by his parents in that time. Their apparent lack of interest in him together with his impending discharge from hospital highlighted a need for social work intervention to prepare them for his return home and so the case was referred to the Children's Judge. At this *audience*, which the parents did not attend, there was sufficient concern for a provisional *Ordonnance de Placement* to be made for six months. André was placed with a foster mother for this period during which time his parents visited him only twice. This elicited further concern and at the next *audience* the judge, recognising the scale of the problem, made a new order that André should be placed under the ASE for two more years during which time he was to remain with the foster mother.

During this period his sister Patricia was born and the *Inspecteur* received reports from the CISS social workers who were worried about the climate of hostility in the home and the lack of parental care. Marie-Claire, the *Inspecteur* requested an *audience* with the judge which, once again, the parents did not attend, and asked for a judicial AEMO for the baby. However, the judge decided that insufficient evidence of danger had been provided by CISS and so ordered a police enquiry. Only after this and a further social work enquiry was a judicial AEMO granted. Over the next few months the CISS social workers met Marie-Claire and reported worrying information about Patricia. If the situation continued they envisaged her going into foster care with her brother. Marie-Claire was pessimistic about the possibilities of keeping the family together and anticipated a placement order being made at the next *audience* as it was clear, or so she felt, that the parents were not and could not fulfil their obligations to the child.

In spite of what, to English eyes, seemed like very clear evidence of parental inadequacy and the consequent need to remove the children from the family the judge's decisions indicated a reluctance to follow this course of action. Instead they demonstrated her desire to give the parents some further opportunities to show interest in André and to care adequately for Patricia. The anticipated placement order was not made but the AEMO was renewed for another year. In addition, the judge asked M. and Mme. Fargeau to visit André more often at his foster mother's and said that André should spend Christmas Day with them at the family home. Perhaps their presence at this *audience* was taken as a sign of their wish for greater involvement with their son. If so, this was not manifested in their other actions although it was subsequently noted that, for the first time, they had a photo of André in their living room.

The judge's readiness to give the parents the benefit of the doubt was not shared by Marie-Claire who disagreed with the judicial decision and felt that vigilance was still needed. In spite of the fact that Patricia was progressing well there were continued causes for concern. The father was unemployed, there was evidence of alcohol and drug abuse in the home and the parents continued to be 'defensive' and difficult to contact. Although the original aim of encouraging regular meetings and better relations between André and his parents was to be pursued, she remained pessimistic about the eventual outcome of the case and thought it was likely that the situation would deteriorate. Her English counterpart had also, at an earlier stage, envisaged adoption as the proper outcome for André, but felt that in spite of the formal aim to reunite the child and his parents, little real work had been done to strengthen the ties betweeen them.

This case highlights several issues that were raised by both the English and the French social workers, concerning adoption in France. These mostly focused on the discrepancy between the intention to keep families together and the reality of repeated short term orders which, in effect, kept them apart; the psychological effects on the child of this unplanned 'drift' into permanency and the damaging consequences of a lack of clear planning for the parents, of whom, one French worker suggested, the impossible was expected.

Although the French workers expressed shock and puzzlement at some of the English attitudes and practices in the field of adoption they also thought that the English system provided the child with more planned possibilities for a secure, stable future outside the natural family. In the French system this alternative was usually arrived at by default.

On the whole adoption in England was viewed as being too easy; not only were adoption procedures started too early, without giving parents sufficient opportunities to change, they were also, in French eyes, too rapid. They found the practice of advertising children for adoption both bizarre and shocking, and the possibility of a child being adopted against the wishes of parents as strange and improper. The willingness of English social workers to place siblings in different adoptive families also puzzled their French counterparts. An English family placement worker, Carol, actively sought a permanent placement for 12-year-old Colin away from his siblings. He and his family had a history of social work intervention for neglect and suspected sexual abuse, and Carol felt that he needed the individualised love and attention of a placement away from them all, if he was to have any chance of blossoming. Whereas she could envisage the positive outcome of such a separation, in French eyes this further splitting-up of the family was unthinkable.

On the other hand, French workers viewed the English practice of open adoption positively and were interested in the thorough preparation that children and their prospective parents received in, for example, the form of life story books. In France, as we have seen, *adoption simple*, the equivalent of open adoption, is rare; more typically, adoption involves a change of name and the severance of all ties with the natural family and the child's past, including the destruction of records. With babies this is possible but for children beyond infancy this break with the past would be impossible to achieve, other than in official terms. Older children in France thus have fewer opportunities for some sort of stable family life if their own families cannot cope. As we will see later in this chapter, residential care, in contrast to England, is a valued alternative to the natural family for older children such as these.

This presents us with an interesting paradox, for whilst the French system privileges the family over the individual child, it is the natural family, not any family, that is seen to be the keystone of society. Thus a child, if it cannot stay in its own family, is seen as being better off in no family. On the other hand, the English system which prioritises the rights of the individual child sees a permanent solution lying in some family rather than none at all.

Clearly, both systems reflect different cultural attitudes towards the natural family but they also share a common focus on families as the best places for children to be brought up, if possible. Once again we see the differences in practice between the two countries lying not in absolutes but in diverging notions of what is ideal, acceptable and possible in the 'real world'.

Foster care

This broad consensus about the importance of families for children is manifested in the frequent use that both systems make of fostering as an alternative to the natural family. In France however, the reluctance to place children permanently extends to an avoidance of long term fostering which is seen as jeopardising the reunification of the family. Short term foster placements are preferred; they are thought of as temporary, leading towards, not away from, the reintegration of the natural family. Nevertheless, in reality, the child may experience several years away from its parents. This may come about in a number of ways. For example, although the placement order may be for six months, the possibilities of it being repeatedly renewed mean that a series of 'temporary' placements accumulate into a long stay in another family. In the case of Sophie, as with that of André, the child may spend more of its early life with a foster family than with its natural parents.

Sophie was placed in a residential nursery at the age of four months, after the unexpected death of her twin sister and remained there, with her mother's agreement, for a year. Although Mme. Gilet visited her daughter regularly after the provisional order was renewed (six months into the placement), she still seemed reluctant to have Sophie back. After a gap of three months without a visit, the case was referred back to the Children's Judge. At this *audience* an order was made for a two year placement in foster care. At the end of this time Sophie would be legally declared 'abandoned', if her mother persisted in not keeping up contact with her. A report from the *travailleuse sociale de secteur* confirmed that Mme. Gilet was not yet in a position to have her daughter back. Three years later Sophie was still with the foster family. Although considerable progress had been made in developing the links between mother and daughter during this period, such that Sophie's return to her mother was envisaged, it remained uncertain as to when in the future this might happen.

In spite of the apparently blurred edges between short term and long term placements that the cases of Sophie and André highlight, it would be a mistake to class these as illustrations of a 'drift' into permanency. It may be more appropriate to see them as indicators of French optimism that time and the active preparation of all parties concerned – children, natural parents and foster parents – will bring about the desired reunification of the family. Though, where optimism may be unjustified, it is perhaps more a matter of persistence in inducing parents to take up their obligations to their children. As one French worker remarked, "placing children in anything other than short term care erodes the parental function." According to him, longer placements serve to absolve parents of their responsibilities to their children. Shorter placements, on the other hand, act as a continual reminder of them.

The French system of fostering has certain features that underpin both optimism and persistence. As we saw in the case of André, parent-child contact is not only judicially encouraged, it is expected. The translation of this expectation into practice is made easier through the different fostering options that enable children to see their parents regularly. Parents have visiting rights when their children are placed, though the cases of André and Sophie suggest that parents are under no legal obligation to visit them. Children may be placed with a relative, with their grandmother or aunt for example. Most placements involve the use of hébèrgement, where the child stays with its natural parents for a night or more on a regular basis. In some cases this may almost amount to part-time foster care, as in the case of Jerome Chapeau, aged two, who spent two days a week in a foster family and the rest of the time at home. For other children and their parents hebergements might be envisaged in the future if the family situation improves, and overnight stays might be gradually increased over a period of months. In Sophie's case, as the relationship improved between mother and daughter, the time spent together increased. However, this arrangement was not without its problems, particularly for Sophie, who found it difficult to adjust to the two lives that hebergement can involve. Perhaps in her case the problems were compounded by the fact that she had hardly lived with her mother before.

The persistence and optimism of the French system was illustrated in the professional responses to this problem and to the reluctance of Mme. Gilet to have her daughter back. In spite of a lack of maternal interest, adoption was not actively considered. However, the threat of adoption was used by the Inspecteur to induce Mme. Gilet to change her attitude and behaviour towards Sophie. In spite of the difficulties that contact between them brought, the judicial and social work approach was to continue the regular contact. Once Sophie's anxiety had been identified the CMPP were consulted and the intervention strategy was modified to accommodate the child's difficilty in adjusting. The frequency of *hébèrgements* were reduced, for the time being, and the *éducatrice* worked to maintain the links between the two. As Sophie's relationship with her mother gradually improved, visits home became more frequent. This flexible but persistent approach, which also involves the co-operation of foster parents, appeared to be getting results.

In contrast to their responses to adoption in England, French workers felt that the English fostering system was more developed than their own. In particular, they thought that foster parents were better trained, better paid and more involved in cases. Some French workers formed the impression that on this side of the Channel, foster parents have a higher status than their French counterparts and were more frequently consulted by social workers. English workers, too, were of the view that fostering in England is better resourced and organised, possibly because, unlike France, it has become the main alternative to remaining in the natural family.

Residential care

Residential care, as the other alternative to remaining in the family is used in both countries, but with important differences. On this side of the channel it enjoys a mixed, but generally negative, reputation. Over the last two decades residential care has been seen as a poor alternative to family life and is used less and less. In France, it is highly regarded, better resourced and more frequently used than in England.

These differences were reflected in the attitudes and responses of English and French social workers to residential care in the other country. Certain aspects of the French system surprised and shocked the English workers. In particular, the practice of placing babies in residential nurseries, *pouponnières*, caused disbelief and disapproval. From this side of the Channel, where residential nurseries were phased out 20 or so years ago, the possibility that a baby like Sophie Gilet might go into residential care soon after birth, was viewed as being very undesirable. However, the nature of the *pouponnière* is rather different from the regimented institutional care that prompted the move away from residential nurseries in England in the 1970s. In the *pouponnière* the organisation and delivery of care is influenced by attachment theory. What this influence means in practice is that infants receive care which recognises their psychological as well as their physical needs, or is at least designed to do so, in the form of more consistent, one-to-one, personalised attention.

Nevertheless, the use of *pouponnières* further stresses the French imperative that no other parent should become the attachment figure, even in the case of recalcitrant natural parents. In this respect, at least, the family's integrity remains unthreatened even if, in reality, the infant spends long periods of time living away from its parents.

Young children, too, may be placed in residential care, as in the case of the three youngest children of the Ivoire family. The 'degradation of the family system', manifested in neglect, parental conflict and alcoholism, was not improving, in spite of concerted interventions by the *éducateur*, Jean-Paul and the CMPP. After another *audience* with the Children's Judge, the mother was required to follow a course of treatment and both parents were required to see a psychiatrist regularly. Jean-Paul was to work with M. and Mme. Ivoire, on their tendency to play down their problems. If there was still no improvement a placement was envisaged. It is interesting to note that Jean-Paul felt that the judge was letting M. and Mme. Ivoire off the parental hook by not obliging them to take up their responsibilities to their children.

However, a phone call from a neighbour prompted a home visit from social workers, after which Mme. Ivoire was hospitalised. Another judicial hearing was held and, with parental agreement, the three youngest children were placed in a residential home for six months. The oldest child, a boy of 11, was to live for the time being with his maternal grandmother. In spite of regular meetings between Jean-Paul and the parents, to prepare them for their children's return and *hebergement* arrangements, whereby the children were home at weekends, the situation did not improve. Although M. and Mme. Ivoire wanted their children back, she was reluctant to have treatment for her alcoholism and both seemed to be unable or unwilling to take steps to improve the situation. Moreover, they were proving to be more and more difficult to meet. Towards the end of the six month placement the team met the parents to let them know of their concerns and of their intention to ask for an extension of the residential placement if things did not improve. At the next hearing the Children's Judge confirmed a further placement for one year.

As with our previous discussions of foster care, we can see from this case that despite intentions to keep the family together, French social workers, like their English counterparts do remove children from the natural family. However, even in this family, where the outlook for improvement looked bleak, it was unlikely that permanent placements would be made. To English eyes this approach appeared to be operating against the interests of the children.

In contrast, for older children, entry into residential care can mark the beginning of a constructive preparation for the future. One of the most noticeable differences in residential care in the two countries is the high priority placed on training in French residential establishments. Young people who cannot remain at home are not merely encouraged but actively enabled to follow a course of vocational training as part of their residential care. As part of this they receive vocational assessment and guidance, as in the example of 15-year-old Sabine Ducroix, (whose case we discussed in Chapter 5), who was recommended to follow a paediatric nurse training by the assessment service. This is followed up by efforts to place the young person in an establishment which offers a suitable training. Caumont, a residential home with forty places, specialises in *restaurant* and the arts of *hotelerie*. There is no real equivalent in England, where these have been reduced to 'catering'. As places are limited and in demand, a selection process operates which matches the young person's aptitude and motivation with the availability of places. In other words, there is competition for placements at Caumont. Given the English experience of residential care this situation presents an ironic contrast with attitudes and practices on this side of the Channel. This difference is further highlighted by the training offered at institutions like Caumont and the responses of the trainees to it. As one might expect in France, training in cookery and the arts of presentation and service of food are taken very seriously by all concerned. This extends from the use of good quality ingredients to the earnest and dignified demeanour of the young trainees who work in the restaurant at Caumont which is open to the public. In comparison, French workers found residential care in England lacking in purpose; young residents seemed apathetic, under-occupied and inactive, and staff appeared anxious not to be seen as directive.

Conclusion

We have seen in this chapter how the idea that families should stay together underpins alternative care in France in several key ways. Firstly it means that placements are rarely permanent; adoption, even for babies, is comparatively rare and long term fostering, if it does occur, is unintended. Placements away from the natural parents are seen as short term and necessary as a stage in the eventual reunification of the family, not as a step towards splitting it up. Residential care is well resourced and valued as a constructive, but temporary, alternative to family life, not as a holding pool. The French system has a number of built-in features which encourage, aid, or if necessary, induce natural parents to care for their children. These include short term placement orders and regular judicial hearings, where parental progress is monitored, parental visiting rights, and *hebergements*, where children spend part of the week at the family home. The strategy of social workers is actively to prepare all parties concerned for the child's return to the family, however distant this may be.

All these features are supported by an optimism that it is possible to recover lost parental function and a persistence in efforts to do so. However, from this side of the Channel, it appears that often these attempts to keep families together achieve more in name than reality. Repeated short term placements and an unwillingness to place children permanently means that not only do some children, in effect, spend more time away from the natural family than within it but also that their futures are, in the long term, uncertain. Nevertheless, what we have also seen in some cases, which in England would have been classed as hopeless, is that this combined optimism and persistence paid off. Whereas here social work efforts would have been directed towards placing the children permanently, in France work aimed at developing the relationships between parents and children enabled these to improve enough for family reunification to be envisaged in the near future.

One aspect of fostering and adoption practice particularly puzzled French and English workers. In contrast to England, foster placement in France is not guided by consideration of the ethnicity of either the child or its potential parents. As we will see in Chapter 10, the very different ideas in France about the relationship between the state and its citizens, mean that their ethnicity is seen as secondary to their French citizenship. Assimilation and social insertion are therefore accorded more importance than cultural or racial diversity. This extends to adoption and fostering practices. According to one French worker, things are different, in this respect, in France "because here everyone is the same". Providing they meet the usual criteria, it appears that any parent can foster any child, as in the case of Sophie Gilet, who was placed with orthodox Jewish foster parents. The French worker in this case was puzzled at what she saw as the preoccupation on this side of the channel with racial matching, at the expense, in her view, of other more important psychological factors. Her English counterpart, on the other hand, was surprised at the apparent absence, in French adoption and fostering practices, of any consideration of the development of 'racial identity'.

Chapter 7: A View from Abroad

Introduction

The preceding chapters have used French cases to look at what happens in France, and how it happens. this chapter draws on the English and French social workers' reflections to highlight the complex differences between the two child protection systems. English social workers, while by no means uncritical of many aspects of French practice, were favourably impressed by the French system, to the point of being envious. The French, although impressed by many aspects of the English way of working and indeed in a number of cases making direct practical application to their own practice, seemed overall to feel content with their own system.

Why should this be? This chapter attempts to disentangle some of the observations of the participants, and some apparent contradictions.

Power and authority

English social workers were seen, and saw themselves, as at once powerful and powerless. Anne-Marie commented, "Eileen is in a way all powerful and yet at the same time she is very much on her own." The English social workers saw French social workers as both less and more powerful than themselves. On the one hand, the judge made many of the decisions that would be made by social workers in England. On the other, as Cathy commented, "the French social worker is more her own agent, making more decisions and using management as advisors." Views about the power of the French social workers were sometimes modified over the course of the research. James, at the beginning of the research, said, "I was left with an impression of greater formality as well as authority attached to his social work role." At the end his comment was that "Jean-Paul worked by consensus not authority. negotiation and persuasion rather than monitoring and checking." These two observations seem to be invoking slightly different notions of authority, but taken together, they give an idea of the complexities of what was being described.

Catherine noted that in England "the magistrate launches the case and then stops.... the (social work) service seems to be charged with making decisions, it's in their power. Before, I thought that the impact of the legal procedure (in England) was very important. For us, from start to finish the judge is involved." This observation locates power with the service rather than the individual social worker, and this view would be supported by Eileen's experience of herself as powerless, and Anne-Marie's comment on this.

Overall, the conclusion of the English social workers is that French social workers have less power, because so much power is held by the judge; but also more authority, partly because this is transmitted by the judge. However, this is also connected to the general level of consensus about the proper role of parents. As a result, social workers in France are better respected, and respect themselves more than their English counterparts. This was remarked on by Vickie, and by Bob in relation to the prevention team. He felt that the workers in the prevention team "took themselves seriously" as professionals, and saw themselves as important.

Both English and French social workers see the English as having less confidence in parents. Jean-Paul said that he had the impression that "in England, abusing families are quite quickly marked down, no one reckons much on their ability to change." Mary's view corroborated this; she reflected on the French case that she was following saying "they are allowing Sophie to spend days with her mother. Here the social worker would spend time with Sophie and her mother.... they, the French social workers, have confidence in Mum. Do we act too much like policemen; not trusting parents?"

Initially a number of the English participants were struck by the fact that French parents were not present at discussions of their case in the CISS and that they did not see the reports written about them by the professionals. They were even more taken aback to discover that parents could be taken to court, and orders could be made, without evidence of harm to the child. This seemed to add up to an authoritarian and dictatorial system. These views were considerably modified during the course of the research as the English social workers began to gain a deeper understanding of the interactions. The English social workers began to question their own assumptions about what 'empowered' parents, and reflect on the discomfort that they all felt about the position of parents at case conferences. Ruth wondered "how the systems in both countries justify the way in which they include or exclude parents. In England do we include parents as a way of avoiding the development of professional skills, of minimizing the difficulties of the task? Is it through discomfort with authority?" Viv noted the contradiction that "our system is less 'judgemental', but parents feel they can't win, they feel powerless."

To begin with, the English social workers saw the French judge as paternalistic. Peter saw the judge who was involved with Sabine Ducroix as taking the role of a grandfather, intervening and making demands which other people then had to see were carried out. The combination of power and direct authority vested in one person, and the lack of need for evidence, all seemed to the English social workers to add up to a paternalistic approach to families which the English system had been at pains to move away from. Although this continued to form part of their perception of the judge, their experience of the reality modified this view. James noted that there could be battles and disagreements between the social worker, or the ASE *Inspecteur* and the judge, and that although the judge had the ultimate power, there was room for argument and negotiation.

Several of the English social workers attended a judge's *audience*, and others heard accounts of how an *audience* had passed off in the cases they were following. There was surprise at the compliance of families and their attitude to the judge. Vickie remarked on a family's ability to have a rational discussion with the judge even when they disagreed with him. Viv pondered on the reasons for this compliance.

"The use of authority by the judge and the family's compliance is very striking. Perhaps it's different when the authority and the message to the parents are all located in, emanate from, one person, the judge. In England, clients resent being asked to do things by people who don't know them."

She wondered if parents did as the judge asked them because they received a more positive message? In contrast, James was struck by the power of parents, both in terms of their rights, and the respect given to their parental authority by the judge. He noted that in one case the parents had the right to choose whether their child should be in a foster placement or residential placement, and that although their decision could be over-ridden by the judge (and only by the judge), he did not in this instance do so. Several of the participants remarked on the importance of parents in France having the ability to prevent their child being adopted.

Another aspect of the compliance of French families was the lack of aggression faced by French social workers. English social workers remarked on the absence of security measures at the French social work offices. Conversely, French social workers were struck by the proliferation of security measures at English offices. The level of aggression faced by English social workers was puzzling to the French workers and they explained this as related to the need for English social workers to find evidence and prove parental failure. Jeanne asked whether "the relationships between families and social workers in England are more aggressive because of the police involvement?"

The role of the police

In France the role of the police in child protection does not bring them into much contact with social workers and they are involved in fewer cases. Even so, there were a number of cases where the police had been involved, either in initial investigations or where there were allegations of sexual abuse committed by adults. The French social workers were interested in both these aspects of the police involvement in England. While Jeanne had seen police involvement as possibly contributing to the difficulties of relationships between social workers and families, other French social workers were able to see some benefits. Two of them thought that there was an advantage in the involvement of the police in the initial investigation and in the case conference because it underlined the seriousness of the concerns and prevented the parents minimising their problems. The role of the English police in cases of alleged sexual abuse was of great interest to the French social workers. Three of the French cases concerned possible sexual abuse, and in two of them a disclosure was made during the research. Both the social workers concerned had heard about the English practice of liaison with the police, and approached the French police to liaise with them before the child was seen. They were pleased with the results of this and felt that it had been helpful for the children concerned. As a result, they both intended to develop their links with the police further. They were also interested in the use of video recordings to spare the child repeated questioning; but they were puzzled by the fact that these videos could not be shown to child protection conferences. English requirements for evidence, and the rules and regulations relating to this remained difficult for French social workers to comprehend.

The favourable views of liaison with the police, especially in the initial stages of the case, were linked to reflections by several French social workers concerning their need to be more direct and confrontative with families. There was an appreciation of the value of check lists, and the English approach to information gathering and report writing was regarded as rigorous. Michelle said that as a result of her involvement in the research, she would make more use of check lists and be more direct with the families she worked with.

Getting things done

Social workers from both countries remarked on the differences in pace between the two systems. It was not that one was quicker than the other in general, but that at a comparable point in the development of a case, the pace of the two systems was very different. The French workers were struck by the speed with which the English were expected to react to a referral. They felt that English workers were expected to move very fast in collecting information in the initial stages, and that this could lead to misapprehensions, as well as creating an unreflective response in the social worker. This was connected to the view that some of the French workers began to develop, that the task of the English social worker was different from their own; that, in Jean-Paul's words, the English social worker "is a specialist in interviewing, co-ordination and the search for evidence." Both French and English social workers were aware of having different interpretations of risk, and that these different interpretations were very important in determining the nature of the subsequent intervention. As Vickie noted, "theories and opinions about preventive work seemed to be the same, and the way Joseph assessed situations was the same, but our assessments of risk were different."

In this case Joseph considered that the risk of a change of placement was greater than the risk of sexual abuse if the child remained where it was. Vickie could not have taken this line, not because she necessarily disagreed with it, but because the discussion could not have reached this point and neither she nor her managers could have taken the risk of the child being abused. The risk, in other words, was to the social workers as well as to the child. Michelle said:

"They (the English) analyse the situation in terms of the level of indicators of danger. It is the sum of these indicators that will lead to a decision. We too have factors which put us on the alert, but we can perhaps take more risks. From the moment when one feels that there is a possibility of movement in the relationships within the family, one takes the elements of risk into account, but they are not the main focus."

The English saw the French system as offering a faster response than their own in respect of the legal process. As we have seen, the fact that an *audience* would normally take place two to three weeks after it was requested, or if necessary, much sooner, was a product of a different legal process. Most of the English workers commented on the speed and flexibility of the French legal system. Viv also commented on the speed with which French social workers expected families to change; one family was made the subject of a three month administrative AEMO, to see whether they could work and change without recourse to the law. Viv felt that this would not have been thought possible for an English family. The difference here, however, may have concerned different perceptions about what constituted positive change. In other words, the French family may not have been expected to show very much change, whereas an English family whose parenting was being assessed as part of a child protection investigation might have to demonstrate quite substantial changes.

In other respects the English saw the French system as being slow, almost leisurely. There were two aspects to this. In the first place, the social workers were not driven into action by the need to avoid risk. As we have noted, Vickie was struck by the fact that when Joseph had problems in finding a placement for Jonathon, who was at risk of sexual abuse by a friend of his father's, he was able to wait for the right placement on the grounds that the risk to Jonathon of a double move was worse than the risk of abuse; Vickie felt that she would have had to move much more quickly.

Secondly, the need to consult with the many other social workers who might also be concerned in a case, took time. James pondered on the need for Jean-Paul to get the agreement to a child's placement, first from the other social workers involved, then from the parents and finally from the judge.

> "The need to liaise with other professionals slows things down, but shares accountability, which makes for less anxiety.... The slowness doesn't seem to lead to disaster, so maybe that doesn't matter."

What James was identifying, was a different set of ideas about planning and getting things done, in which the process of reaching an agreement was as important as the agreement that was reached.

Another aspect of the pace of work was the question of how the workers paced themselves. The English social workers noted the absence of a duty system in the voluntary agency, and the extent to which even the *assistante sociale* in the CISS was protected from the immediate pressure of unscheduled inquiries. They noted how it was possible for French workers to plan their work and get on with it without interruption; but they also thought that there was a difference of attitude. James said, "We take too much responsibility. They decide their own terms of response." A French Children's Judge saw it much the same way: "Why do English social workers feel so responsible for what happens to families?"

The question of accountability and anxiety leads us back to a consideration of the case conference. The English social workers' comments on the case conference were mainly critical. They tended to see it as a setting which was difficult for both parents and social workers. Cathy regarded it as an important achievement that she had managed to avoid the necessity for a case conference with one of her families. James saw case conferences as places for sharing information but not anxieties. The anxiety was left with the social worker.

The importance of families

A permeating theme so far has been the connection between cultural notions of 'the family' and the attitudes and practices of social workers and others who work with families. In particular, we have highlighted the strong influence that French valorisations of the natural family have had on decisions about separating children from their parents, including the reluctance of judges, *Inspecteurs* and social workers to place children permanently away from their families. In contrast, we have seen how the English emphasis on the rights of the individual child has often been associated with their removal from their family of origin.

In spite of these differences, both place great emphasis on the importance of family life for the healthy development of the child. The differences lie in which kind of family is considered to be best for children. As several French participants noted, French social workers are primarily interested in the quality of family relationships and in the emotional lives of family members. Assessments, therefore, need to be qualitative and sensitive to subtle signs, as in the case of André Fargeau where it was regarded as significant that the parents had placed a photograph of him in their living room for the first time. From this side of the Channel it appeared strange that this gesture was accorded more significance than the failure of his parents to visit his foster placement. According to French workers their English counterparts were too preoccupied with evidence, rather than being open to a variety of possible explanations of the behaviour in question.

The reliance in England on check lists to assess parental adequacy appeared to some French participants to exemplify the English preoccupation with facts and evidence and the attempt to quantify the unquantifiable. On the other hand, some French workers felt that not only would their own work benefit from the rigour and clarity that the use of checklists involved, but that it would be more open and honest towards parents who would have a clearer idea of what was being expected of them.

What is clear from these differences is that there is strong interest, on both sides of the Channel, in parent-child relationships. However, as we will see, although both countries expect that mutual attachment should exist between parents and children, the origins of that relationship are viewed rather differently. English workers felt that the French took for granted the 'natural' link between parents and children and assumed that parenting came naturally because of blood ties, even when there seemed to be very little evidence of this. On the other hand, French workers remarked that the English seemed to assume that parents would never be able to do it if, at the time they were being observed, they were not demonstrating a capacity to do it. One French worker exclaimed, "But, it is only a hypothesis that the mother cannot cope with her son as well as the new baby!" Like other French participants she felt that rather than tackling the deeper causes of parental difficulties, current behaviour was taken as proof of parental inadequacy.

As we noted in Chapter 6, attachment theory has influenced attitudes and practices with children in both countries but, ironically, in ways which both contradict the other country's interpretation and which seem to be at odds with the original theory. In England, the ideas of John Bowlby and Donald Winnicott on the importance of secure attachment in early childhood contributed to the phasing out of residential nurseries and the rise of fostering. The latter was thought to mimic the mother-child relationship and thus be closer to the 'real thing' than the institutional wards and nursing care typical of residential nurseries. In other words foster care was seen as a reasonable alternative to the natural family. However, the impact of short term foster placements and of frequent stays in different foster families, which is the reality for many children in the English system, appears to be at odds with the spirit of attachment theory.

In effect, these children may experience the making and breaking of attachments many times in the first few years of life. The irony of this was not lost on the English workers.

By contrast, in France attachment theory is used to underpin the organisation of infant care outside the natural family in a different way. As we saw in Chapter 6 the French use of residential nurseries, *pouponnières*, shocked English workers, who felt that they could have a damaging developmental effect on children. However, although the *pouponnière* is not the direct equivalent of the erstwhile residential nursery, their use seems to contradict the tenets of attachment theory as much as the English use of foster care. In France, placement in a *pouponnière* is justified on the basis that it offers supplementary rather than alternative attachments to the natural family. Nevertheless, as one English worker remarked, if a baby actually spends more of its early life in a *pouponnière*, than at home, this conception of supplementary attachment becomes difficult to sustain.

At an individual level it was clear that, while workers from both countries employed psychological notions of attachment to understand family relationships, their respective interpretations could be very different. In the case of Sophie Gilet, who spent the first year of her life in a *pouponnière* and the following three in foster care, it was noted by the French worker, a psychologist, that Sophie was exhibiting sexualised behaviour; she wanted to see the *éducatrice*'s breasts and at school she wanted to kiss boys in a sexual way. However, whilst the French worker interpreted this desire for intimacy as a sign of emotional deprivation in early life, her English counterpart felt that, on this side of the Channel, the child's behaviour would have been taken as a sign of early emotional over-stimulation and possibly sexual abuse.

Differences in the interpretation of behaviours were also evident, to French and English workers, when it came to recognising a breakdown in family relationships. As one *éducatrice* remarked, "At the moment when the French would begin to work with the causes, the English assess the parents as incapable and begin the process of separation." Another observed that English decisions seem to reflect a pessimism about the possibilities of change within families. On the whole, French participants thought that English families were not offered enough help in the form of in-depth work and that English social workers had less confidence in the family's capacity to change. One French worker suggested that at the point when she might expect families to be most receptive to change, when they have accepted that they have difficulties in caring for their child, the English envisaged the child's removal from the family.

However, as we have already seen, English workers thought that the French system placed too much value on the natural family at the expense of the child's future security and present safety. Furthermore, they felt that their French counterparts were deluding themselves in assuming that the restoration of family ties was always a desirable goal. The French were not uncritical of their own system and shared some of the misgivings of the English social workers. Some felt that the system expected too much of parents without giving clear enough guidelines. Others thought that contradictory demands were placed upon parents. One *éducateur* described how, in a case where there were strong suspicions about the parents, they were subject to intensive surveillance in the first few months whilst at the same time being expected to trust the social worker. Another French worker suggested that her colleagues were not deluding themselves; they were, in effect, knowingly following two agendas, an official one, which respected parental consent, and another which, recognising that a placement away from the natural family might, in reality, be permanent, chose a foster family with this in mind. Long term fostering, according to a worker who specialised in foster work, does exist in France, but it cannot really be admitted.

French perceptions of the English situation also pointed to contradictions and complications. The French saw that, whilst the English were at pains to find a permanent solution for the child away from an unsatisfactory natural family, this might involve, as in the case of Colin Brown, a number of different temporary placements, more likely to produce instability than security. Moreover, one *éducatrice* wondered whether the efforts of the English workers to defend the rights of the child to a lasting solution properly took into account the suffering of the child in the event of separation. Others remarked that, although the English system does not appear to have a high regard for the natural family, as the higher incidence of adoption here would suggest, children and their natural parents are encouraged, in the case of open adoption, to keep contact. In France, on the other hand, where a much higher value is placed on the natural family, adoption normally involves an irrevocable split. Some French workers felt that, like them, their English counterparts were constrained by the system. For example, some found that English social workers gave more importance to the natural family than they had originally realised but that the English system prevented them from expressing this belief in their practice.

To assume, therefore, that each system is uniform and internally consistent, is mistaken. The observations of these English and French social workers suggest that, on the contrary, inconsistencies and contradictions are part of both countries' practices.

Leaving the system

There were few comments from either English or French social workers about the process or practice of closing cases. The cases with the most definite endings for the English social workers were those which culminated in adoption. French children in foster or residential care seemed to be able to stay in their placements until the age of 21, and would therefore have a long career in the system. There was no expectation in any of the English cases, where the children concerned were younger, that any of them would still be in local authority accommodation when they were 18; adoption was envisaged, even if not thought to be achievable, for all of them. Although the law appeared only briefly in the English cases, the French social workers were surprised that an order could be made for a child of any age that would last, without legal review, until that child was 18.

What made the biggest difference to the overall picture was the fact that most of the French cases involved children who were either still at home, or were working towards rehabilitation with the family. Most of the English cases involved children who were no longer at home and did not expect to return there. In both countries, where children were still at home, there was no great confidence that a closed case would stay closed.

As we indicated at the beginning of this chapter, the French social workers seemed on the whole to be content with their system. They were not, however, uncritical of their way of working, and showed a keen interest in many aspects of the English system and English practice. They showed a readiness to try out new ways of working stimulated by discussion with the English workers, and there did not seem to be any problem for them in accommodating new approaches within their existing organisational structures. Conversely, the English social workers, who were more critical of their own system, seemed less influenced in their practice by what they learned from their French counterparts. This is not to imply that they were impervious to influence; there were many points at which it was clear that English workers were getting a new perspective on their work, and were stimulated and intrigued by this. The problem was rather that there was little flexibility within the system to allow them to try out different approaches. The heavy bureaucratisation of the English system, which was identified by both the English and the French workers, gave very little space for doing things differently.

Perhaps it was not only the inflexibility of their system that made it difficult for the English social workers to borrow and experiment. There was a greater sense of optimism in France about the possibility of change and a greater professional self confidence and a feeling of being valued by clients, colleagues, judges and a wider public. Trying out new ways of working is easier when you are working in a flexible system where your powers and responsibilities do not outrun your authority and when you are working in a cohesive and well-supported team.

English social workers were proud of their professional rigour, their fostering services and their anti-discriminatory practice. Their difficulty was that they felt that they had little control over their work and that their contribution to the well-being of children and young people at risk or in danger was seriously undervalued.

Section Three
Politics, Policy and Ideology

Chapter 8: The Politics of Child Protection

Viewed from Britain, one of the most surprising features of the French child protection system is the apparent absence of political and media hostility to the social workers who staff it. Few child abuse scandals grab the headlines in the popular press and no social workers have been pilloried at public enquiries for their alleged incompetence.

But although French children are injured and abused by adults, and French social workers are sometimes prosecuted for incompetence, the 'institutionalised' animosity and mistrust of social workers, so familiar in Britain since the late 1970s, is effectively absent (Colombani 1981, Hocquenhem 1983, Regnault 1994). While this hostility found its most vehement expression in Britain in the period after 1979, the origins of these very different attitudes can be traced back to the 17th and 18th centuries. It was in this period that the two different philosophies, which describe a very different relationship between the law, the state and the individual and underpin subsequent social and fiscal policies, emerged. As we have seen, these differences have shaped both the public portrayal of social workers in the two countries and the roles they are required to play.

Optimistic and pessimistic philosophies

The central idea to emerge from the European Enlightenment and the French revolutions of 1789 and 1848 was that rather than simply living in accordance with the precepts of history, human beings could 'make' history; they could transform themselves and transcend their circumstances. Michel Foucault (1986) in his essay *What is Enlightenment? (Was ist Aufklärung?)* argues that above all, the Enlightenment brought into being an 'attitude', a way of understanding and thinking about the world, which had not existed before and which he describes as 'modern'.

"To be modern is not to accept oneself as one is in the flux of the passing moments, it is to take oneself as object of a complex and difficult elaboration: what Baudelaire, in the vocabulary of the day, calls *dandysme* ... Modern man, for Baudelaire, is not the man who goes off to discover himself, his secrets and his hidden truth; he is the man who tries to invent himself. This modernity does not 'liberate man in his own being'; it compels him to face the task of producing himself."

This modern consciousness was characterised by the capacity for self consciousness and the related possibility of self-realisation; that one might be able to become the person one wished to be. Thus human beings, rather than being simple objects of historical processes could, together, make and remake the world in accordance with the dictates of reason rather than tradition. The belief that ideas could be the motor of change and that collective action and state intervention could forge a better world were the lived experience of mainland Europeans.

But in Britain, while there was no actual revolution, monarchs lived in fear of it and the 'optimistic' ideas which had inspired it. What we see instead is the rise to dominance of a very different, 'pessimistic', Utilitarian philosophy which continues to underpin British law, politics and policy. Utilitarianism grows out of the ideas of Thomas Hobbes (1588–1679) who strove, amongst other things, to develop an apologia for absolute monarchy. As R. S. Peters (1989) writes:

"Hobbes thought that a multitude of men became a common-wealth by the device of authority in which men gave up unlimited self-assertion against each other – their 'rights of nature' – and authorised a man or a body of men to act on their behalf. This 'social contract', which was presupposed by sovereignty, was a consequence of the overwhelming fear of death which haunted men in a state of nature. Hobbes also deduced from this 'ideal experiment' that such a sovereign must be absolute, the sole reason for the institution of government being the safety of the people." (p.135)

In this Hobbesian world, all the subjects of the sovereign, by dint of the threat they pose to each other's lives and property, become potential adversaries. The liberty of one subject constantly threatens to impose a limitation on the liberty of another. Their safety is vouchsafed by their subjugation to a sovereign whose power is used entirely negatively; to suppress the threat to the lives and property of the subjects and to maintain social order. As such, Utilitarianism is profoundly conservative, a philosophy of stasis and a rationale for the maintenance of an unchanging set of hierarchical social relationships. It is opposed to official attempts to effect individual or social change or betterment and, as such, it provides the cornerstone for contemporary radical right-wing libertarian politics and minimalist or non-interventionist approaches to 'social problems'.

In French post-revolutionary politics, by contrast, other citizens emerge as the pre-condition for individual liberty and social progress. In overthrowing the ancient regime they have learnt how to make history rather than simply live in accordance with its dictates. Thus, the freedom and progress of each citizen is contingent upon the freedom and progress of all citizens. In this scheme citizens emerge not as adversaries but as collaborators. The individual citizen does not surrender a portion of their freedom to the state, because together they are the state. This idea has a familiar ring, of course, since as the historian A. J. P. Taylor (1976) has observed, while Karl Marx took his philosophy from Germany and his economics from Britain, it was in France that he learned his politics.

Whether either of these philosophies is 'right' or desirable is less important for us than the fact that they have left an indelible mark upon the social policies and social practices of the two nations.

Philosophy, social policy and the family in France

Commaille (1994) observes that:

> "The family, as Portalis has said emerges as 'the seed bed of the state, the cradle of the state, for domestic virtues are of the same strain as the virtues of citizenship'. If familialism has had and continues to have so much value at the core of French society, this is because the family has been given an essential role within the social and political structure of society." (p.129)

He notes that "French 'familialism' stands in marked contrast with the English obsession to preserve 'privacy' ". The origins of modern French family policy are usually traced back to the emergence of the 'social question' in 19th century France. The social question concerned the impact of industrialisation and rapid social change on the family and was asked by a group of Catholic employers who, encouraged by the promulgation of the encyclical Rerum Novarum of Pope Leon XIII in 1891, devised a system of supplementary wages to support families in discharging their responsibilities. This system, based on the voluntary participation of individual businesses, expanded over time until, in 1932, a law was passed which required all businesses to participate in the scheme. In 1938 another law established unified conditions of eligibility and standardisation of family allowances.

An abiding national concern with the birth-rate, rooted in anxieties about past and impending wars and invasions, found expression in the creation of the 'Family Code' in July 1939. The 'Family Code' extended family allowance benefits, gave mothers a substantial grant for the birth of their first child, an allowance if they stayed at home with their children and significant financial rewards if they produced three or more children. Post-war legislation in 1945 and 1946 extended and consolidated these benefits.

By this process, the family in France came, in the post-war period, to be the central object of French social policy. In 1992 France devoted 4% of its GDP to family benefits, putting it amongst the top five nations in Europe. However, like many other Western European countries in the mid-1990s, France is tending to move away from a focus upon 'the family' towards a concentration upon social problems encountered by particular families and individuals.

Nonetheless, familialism has lost none of its ideological potency in France, and political commitment to it transcends party political differences. The communist left presents the family as a social entity under threat from poor social conditions. The non-communist left favours 'individual freedom' and limitations on the scope of state intervention. On the question of the family however it operates the 'doctrine of the double negation', espousing both non-interference and non-indifference (Johanet G. 1982).

The new right, 'modern aid' faction, argues that support for families must be tailored to modern economic conditions. As such it offers a remarkably muted version of Anglo-American new right thinking on the family. The conservative right, in tune with the Catholic Church, is hostile to any 'freedoms' which threaten moral breakdown and call the institution of the family into question. They identify the family as 'the material and primary institution', 'the actor in social and political activity' and 'the keeper of national values'. On the far right the family is identified with the nation, and governmental support for a high birth rate is seen as an essential bulwark against immigration and a dilution of the national essence.

Philosophy, social policy and the family in Britain

If the 'family' in France is a "public issue", in Britain, at an ideological level at least, it is emphatically a "private trouble" (Mills 1959). Whereas in France the 'family' and its future is a legitimate concern of governments and an appropriate target for state policy, in the UK political responses to the 'family' are characterised by a deep ambivalence. In French law and policy, families are the building blocks which constitute the state. In UK law and policy, the 'individual' stands apart from the state. In French child care law the idea of the state and the family are indissoluble. In British child care law the individual and the state are potential adversaries whose interests are effectively irreconcilable. It is for these reasons that Britain has no explicit 'family policy'.

"There is a contradiction between the belief that the State should not encroach upon the autonomy of the family and its perceived duty to ensure that family care of dependents and socialisation of the young is adequately conducted. By acting indirectly, abstaining from proclamation of general objectives for the family, and intervening only against families which can be defined as malfunctioning or in need, the State has been able to minimise controversy regarding its intrusions." (Chester 1994, p.227)

Indeed, it is in the area where the state is most likely to intervene 'against' families believed to be 'malfunctioning' – child protection – that the usually unspoken 'controversy' about the relationship between the family and the state in Britain finds expression. Arguably, it is precisely because no 'general objectives for the family' have been 'proclaimed' that the controversy in this area is so vociferous.

Chester highlights the negative connotation ascribed to social intervention, whether at the level of social policy or social work practice. But the inevitable effect of this non-interventionist stance is to identify, by default, those 'against' whom the state must intervene as pathetic or pathological. This perspective sits very uneasily with the commitment to 'partnership' and 'normalisation' embodied in the 1989 Children Act. Indeed, it is the argument of this book that the positive potential of the Children Act has been subverted in part by the neo-utilitarian orthodoxy which currently holds sway both in government and in the broader political culture.

This view of the state-family relationship, while it derives from traditional philosophical and political beliefs and has always been present, only began to gain its current strength in the country in the 1970s. At other times, in Britain as in France, other governments have pursued positive policies which have located families which are subject to state intervention not as a mere pathological or pathetic residue who place a burden upon the body politic, but as people whose destinies are linked with our own and whose economic and social well-being should be vouchsafed by the state.

British social work in the post war period

In his influential book, *The Social Worker*, published in the mid-1930s, Clement Attlee, who subsequently became the first post-war Labour Prime Minister, identified social work as the mechanism whereby a future welfare state would adapt to the ever-changing needs of its citizens. He argued that the social worker should not only work with family problems but act as a pathfinder or scout for the welfare state, identifying new social problems and social needs. In response, an expanding welfare state would develop new social policies and new social services. These developments were to be part of the broader, egalitarian, project of the redistribution of wealth and opportunity to which the Labour Party was committed.

The first Labour government of the 1940s and early 1950s concentrated on the development of universal provision: the national health service, occupational and health insurance and secondary education for all. It was therefore left to the second Labour administration of Harold Wilson, elected in 1964, to "complete the work of the welfare state" through the development of an integrated system of personal social services. As with the earlier reforms of the 1940s, these developments were influenced profoundly by social scientists, the social work profession and politically sympathetic senior civil servants with a shared view of the relationship which should obtain between social work, the state and the family.

As Parton (1991) has noted:

> "The consensus which underpinned the growth of child care social work during this period had a number of dimensions. It was assumed that the interests of the social worker, and hence the state, were similar to, if not the same as, the clients they were trying to help." (p.20)

Thus between 1964 and 1970 we witnessed the rapid expansion and professionalisation of British social work, culminating in the creation of a national system of local authority Social Services Departments in 1970. Alongside these administrative developments came legislation which sought to transfer previously unprecedented powers from central government to local government and from the law to social work (Pitts 1988).

The political alliances developed by social work in the 1950s and 60s account for the different size and scope of social work in the two countries and the concentration of social workers in 'social work' agencies, in Britain, rather than in multi-disciplinary teams in a variety of organisations and agencies as in France. This is also why the professional identity of social work appears to be far stronger in Britain than in France. In Britain, this identity has been supported through the development of large professional associations, a national 'trade press', the proliferation of 'learned journals' and the location of professional training primarily in the university sector. Whereas in England and Wales social work has attained most of the trappings of a profession, in France it remains an activity which complements the efforts of other professionals and non-professionals in a broader range of settings.

But as Cooper (1993) and Parton (1991) have argued, the influential relationship between social work and the state was not "organic" to British political culture. Rather, social work had a unique relationship with the Wilson administration of 1964, and the duration of its influence was determined by the duration of that administration. From the mid-1970s, the political power and influence of social work declined steadily.

The political affiliations of social work in France are very different. As we have seen, the importance of state support for 'the family' is a central tenet of the programmes of all the major political parties, particularly the parties of the right. In addition, the fundamentally different conception of the relationship between the family and the state means that the objectives of professional social work in France, the maintenance of family relationships and social cohesion, are congruent with both the dominant political ideologies and popular discourse.

Under Mitterand's presidency in the 1980s, the social work role was broadened to encompass a national programme of social prevention and insertion for 'socially marginal' young people. This initiative was inspired in large part by concerns about the integration of young people of North and Central African origin into the mainstream of French cultural and economic life (Bonnemaison 1982, King 1986). One of the major differences between French and British social policy and social work in the 1980s was the increased interventionism of the former and the attempted withdrawal from the 'social' sphere by the latter.

Welfare eclipsed

The mid-1960s in the USA had seen the emergence of a politically powerful 'back to justice' movement which was part of a broader, critique of state intervention in the lives of individuals, and 'welfarist' social policies. These arguments began to make an impact on British political and academic life in the mid-1970s signalling, as they did, a widespread disillusionment with the capacity of the state to 'do good'. Protagonists maintained that any system which attempted to fuse a concern with the 'welfare' of the child with a concern for 'justice' must inevitably fail to deliver justice. The solution proposed by the 'back to justice' lobby was that whenever and wherever possible we should 'leave the kids alone'. 'Radical Non-Intervention' was born.

This was a significant moment in the relationship between social work, the law and the state because it challenged the two central assumptions upon which that relationship had been based. The assumption that the social work presence in the system would benefit the child was supplanted by the proposition that the social worker might well be part of the problem. The assumption that the socially deprived child or family should be protected from exposure to the legal system was supplanted by the idea that the law, and lawyers, were there to defend the rights of families and children against the incursions of agents of the state, namely, social workers.

The Short Report

These concerns informed the deliberations of the All-Party Social Services Committee of the House of Commons, chaired by the Labour MP Renee Short, which reported in 1984. Short was concerned about the relationship between the rights of children and the rights of parents and how, in safeguarding the one, we might be infringing the other. It was concerned about perceived imbalances of power in decision-making about children between courts and local authorities and the movement, over the previous decade, away from residential care as a solution to family problems.

While not denying the importance of rights, Short recognised the inherent danger that a separation of rights from duties runs the risk of unnecessarily projecting each of the parties to child care proceedings into an adversarial relationship with the others. The report notes:

> "If more consideration were given to the respective respon-sibilities of state, parents and child, the issues might be seen in more positive and less divisive terms." (para 15)

While Short identifies state intervention in the business of the family as a "last resort" it also recognises that it is, overwhelmingly, the poor who enter public care and that the state should therefore pursue a broad-based preventive strategy which strives to make good the material and personal deficits experienced by child and family.

Parton writes:

> "The emphasis on prevention was the fundamental base for developing sensitive, supportive and participative services where the interests of the child in the context of the family could be provided for." (p.31)

Short also strove to achieve a proper balance between the claims of 'welfare' and the claims of 'justice' by delineating those matters which fell within the purview of the law and those which were the proper business of social workers.

> "The general principle on which we have based our consideration of the correct balance between the need for justice and the welfare interests of children is that the court should make long-term decisions impinging directly on the rights and duties of children and their parents, and that the local authority or other welfare agency should make decisions on matters which, although they may be of equal or greater importance, are not susceptible to clear unambiguous resolution. It is then a question of defining into which category each class of decision falls." (para.67)

The report indicated that because the question was not about whether 'welfare' or 'justice' should prevail, but rather about how the legitimate claims of each might be most effectively met, the decision-making process should be less formally legalistic, and 'inquisitorial' rather than 'adversarial'. This new forum was to be known as a 'Family Court'.

The 1985 Review of Child Care Law

In its recommendations to the Review of Child Care Law (1985) the Short Report attempted to keep alive a thoughtful social democratic "interventionism" in the face of an increasingly strident doctrinaire demand for non-intervention emanating from the political right. However, as Parton (1991) observes:

> "... the Review was not convinced by the argument that any changes to the substantive law and procedure could only be effective in the context of the introduction of the Family Court System. 'On the contrary we can see some logic in a prior consideration of law.' (para. 2.30) In this respect, the Review

departed from the Short Report. This issue was to surface again during the passage of the Children Bill in 1989. (p.27)

The Review emphasised the need for the greater use of a strengthened Supervision Order, with greater powers over both parents and children, instead of Care Orders for children who were "Home on Trial". The Review attempted to extend the range of options available to the Court but to 'normalise family relations' while offering protection to the child. While the responsibilities of social work were expanded, their powers were circumscribed and the subordination of social work to the dictates of the Court was underscored.

Jasmine Beckford and the legal annexation of child care social work

In December 1985 the findings of the Public Inquiry, chaired by Louis Blom-Cooper Q.C., into the death of Jasmine Beckford at the hands of her father were published. The report, *A Child In Trust*, was unequivocal in its ascription of responsibility for this tragedy:

> "Jasmine ... became the victim of persistent disfunctioning social work while the law demanded, above all, her protection." (p.127)

What was at issue, the report maintained, was not just the actions of particular social workers in a particular case, but a "widespread" social work culture which, it asserted, was based upon the "rule of optimism and natural love". The tragedy occurred, it seemed, not because of deficiencies in the system or some of its agents but because of deficiencies in the beliefs and attitudes which underpinned the practices of an entire profession. The report suggested that social workers were going about their task in wilful ignorance of their legal responsibilities and with scant regard for the realities of the lives of endangered children.

Thus, to the popular stereotype of social workers as morally and politically deviant was added the notion that, because of their gross incompetence, they were dangerous as well. Whether intervening too readily and endangering families, or too late and endangering children, social work was represented as a threat. This was a threat, moreover, which could only be contained by the law and a revitalised management.

The stress on the key role of 'managers' in curbing the excesses, or monitoring the shortcomings, of professionals in child protection social work fed into the burgeoning managerialism which was beginning to assert itself in statutory social work agencies in the mid-1980s (Clarke et al 1994). Blom-Cooper's nod in the direction of "managers" undoubtedly accelerated the bureaucratisation of the professional task and gave impetus to the proceduralisation of child care assessments via, "predictive", check-lists (Greenland 1987).

The subordination of social work professionalism to social work managers was, as we have seen, paralleled by the further subordination of social work to the law in the 1985 Review of Child Care Law. This was a move which was keenly supported by social work's professional validating body, CCETSW, in its *Law Report* (Ball et al 1988). The report observes that:

> "In a profound sense, therefore, the law is both the bed-rock of social work practice, and the touchstone by which its actions must ultimately be judged." (p.11)

In the wake of this report a Law examination and a 'competencies' model of assessment, featuring a wealth of check-lists and schedules, became a mandatory part of pre-professional social work education.

Social work at bay

By the mid-1980s hostility to social work in Britain was widespread. The political right indicated the social work presence as something which undermined the rule of law by allowing consideration of irrelevant personal and social circumstances. Those in the political centre, the civil libertarians, cited social work as a prime example of the tendency of state agencies to make unwarranted incursions into the lives and liberties of citizens and to snatch away the children of the poor because their families failed to conform to middle class standards of hygiene or propriety. For them and the right, social workers were agents of creeping totalitarianism. Somewhat paradoxically, the critique from the political left had echoes of both of these positions but in addition indicted social work as the 'velvet glove' disguising the 'iron fist of capitalist oppression'.

Thatcherism and social work

These themes accorded closely with the neo-Utilitarian commitments of the first Thatcher administration of 1979. The intellectual underpinning of this administration was derived in large part from the work of Karl Popper (1945) and Frederick Hayeck (1944).

Popper and Hayeck maintained that the "welfare state" represented the "thin end" of the totalitarian "wedge" and, using the analogies of Nazism and Soviet Communism, argued that the "social engineering" represented by the "welfare state" would lead inevitably to a loss of freedom. In liberal democracies, they suggest, the law represents the last line of defence for the individual against the totalitarian state. In this argument, social work is located in the vanguard of the forces struggling to bring that totalitarian state into being.

The fact that British social work had carved out a relatively large domain for itself and a comfortable and rewarding political relationship with the Labour Party made it an obvious target for a radical right wing government with a hostility to the professions in general and those concerned with social intervention in particular. Social work and the academic social sciences which served it were viewed by the Thatcher administration with deep suspicion because not only were they interfering in 'family business', they were also insinuating imported, 'social' and sexual ideas into British culture.

The Thatcher government wanted to create a Britain in which self-sufficient families with more of their own money in their pockets would take back control of their lives, and those of their children, from the interfering 'nanny state' and its agents. However, this vision fitted uneasily with the reality of Britain in the 1980s. This was the decade in which unemployment soared to an unprecedented three million, Britain's industrial base was drastically reduced and the post-war tendency towards the narrowing of the gap between the incomes of the rich and the poor was reversed. This was also the decade which witnessed an unprecedented 17% rise in births out of wedlock and escalating divorce rates. It was the decade in which we discovered that far from being a 'haven in a heartless world', for women and children, the home was a place in which they were most vulnerable to assault and abuse. These were some of the factors which led more and more commentators in the mid-1980s to conclude that the British family faced a 'moral crisis'.

The political response of the Thatcher government, the popular press and most political and moral commentators to this contradiction at the core of Thatcherism was to blame social workers, left-wing school teachers and lax parents for undermining family values and encouraging deviant lifestyles. This condemnation found expression at both national and local government levels through the imposition of far greater bureaucratic, administrative and legal controls upon employees of the state.

The hijacking of the 1989 Children Act

It was hardly surprising therefore that the innovative and progressive elements at the core of the 1989 Children Act were obscured by the flight into spurious legal, and administrative certainties which became the hallmark of child protection practice in Britain in the 1980s. The 1989 Act was designed to promote a coherent system of preventive work as well as clear and effective procedures for the investigation and processing of child protection allegations. It aimed to enhance relationships between the voluntary and statutory spheres and to free them to operate in ways which allowed the realisation of their full potential. In the event, the preventive, 'social', 'developmental' and 'therapeutic' objectives of the Act were subverted by legal and administrative imperatives. The social work profession, battered by a series of highly publicised public enquiries and a mauling from the tabloids worthy of a Labour leader on the eve of a general election, offered no resistance. The Act was, instead, prest into the service of a child protection system dominated by lawyers and managers. As Chester (1994) has observed:

> "Ideological critiques may have found particular opportunities for influence in a period when earlier political consensus was breaking up, as happened in the UK during the 1970s and 1980s."

Legal annexation

Michael King (1991) argues that in the 1980s the social work role in the English child protection system was 'annexed' by the law, thus transforming social workers into agents of the legal system; preoccupied with questions of 'evidence' and 'proof' to the detriment of considerations of 'need' and 'suffering'. The extension of rights embodied in the 1989 Act was, of course, also an extension of the sphere of operations of the law and marked an important shift of power, autonomy and political and professional influence away from social work, towards the legal profession. King points to:

> "The law's propensity to 'enslave' other discourses or produce hybrid or bastard discourses of dubious validity." (p.8)

As a result of this enslavement, it is only those bits of social scientific knowledge which echo the common-sense individualism of law which can be assimilated into the hybrid discourse. Having once been assimilated, this knowledge is purged of its subtlety and ambiguity, and proceduralised (Habermas 1971). Thus, when social scientific theory or research findings enter the courtroom, they do so not as a contribution to a better understanding of the factors at work in a particular social situation, but as "evidence".

Thus potted theory and research findings are presented as "theory evidence", often offered in support of incomplete "fact evidence". This attempt to use theory in the same way a drunk uses a lampost, for support rather than illumination, illustrates very well the excesses wrought by legal annexation (Cracker 1976).

Managerial annexation

At the same time, the social work role was also being annexed from within by 'managerialism'. In the mid-1980s, social workers whose job it had originally been to seek out and devise solutions to social problems were pushed to one side by professional managers who identified their primary task as the 'delivery' of 'tightly targeted' cost-effective services to their 'customers'. Managerialism concerns itself with the detail of policy, practice, beliefs and values in an organisation. It is concerned with individual customers or 'service-users', and this concern extends neither beyond that person's contractual involvement with the organisation not to similarly afflicted individuals who have no such involvement. As Clarke et al (1994) observe, however, managerial annexation does not mark the complete demise of what they describe as bureau professionalism in social work, but its transformation:

> "Thus we would argue that the survival of bureau-professionalism in a variety of organisational settings is not just an idiosyncratic hangover from the old regime; nor does it always constitute residual pockets of countervailing power. It is a necessary component of the new; what is at stake is not the eradication of bureau-professionalism but the degree to which relevant clusters of skills and values can be subordinated to, and accommodated within, the new political and organisational logics embodied in managerialism." (p.233)

Managerialism echoes the minimal statism of Thatcherism and the radical non-intervention espoused by the back to justice movement. As a result, in the 1980s interventions by managers which aimed to limit the involvement of welfare professionals in people's lives came to assume the mantle of radicalism while practitioners who insisted on seeking out new "needs" were portrayed as reactionaries. (Dennington and Pitts 1991).

Deprofessionalisation

As a consequence, British social workers in the spheres of child care and child protection spent less and less time exercising professional discretion and more and more following managerial guidelines, completing check-lists and searching for legally admissible evidence with which to brief solicitors. The effect of this was a significant deprofessionalisation of the social work task.

Yet even as their professional authority was being eroded, the power shifts and redesignation of roles occasioned by these developments, and crystallised in the 1989 Children Act effectively handed social workers in England and Wales the responsibility for the investigation and, in effect, the prosecution of child protection proceedings. This generated a great deal of anxiety.

Chapter 9: Protecting Social Workers: Child Protection, Media Abuse and the Organisational Dynamics of Anxiety

Fortress social work

When French social workers participating in our study first walked through the doors of a London Area Office they were astounded by the fortress atmosphere of the reception area – protective glass, security locks and video cameras. The author of this chapter worked for several years in an inner London social services neighbourhood office which prided itself on its close community links and commitment to innovative preventative practices, not least in child protection work (Cooper 1987). But in the mid-1980s many of the hitherto stable underpinnings of English social work were about to give way. The fallout from the Jasmine Beckford report (London Borough of Brent, 1985) and the subsequent spate of highly publicised child deaths changed the face of child protection work. The complexity of these changes was hard to assimilate at the time, but in retrospect it is clear that the primary force acting on the social work profession then, and since, has been anxiety. Sometime in 1986 a violent incident occurred in the reception room of our neighbourhood office. At a team meeting the following day someone called for the urgent introduction of a protective screen on the reception counter. There was little dissent and the work was soon completed. An office which had striven to be accessible to its public, to balance the complex equation of care and control in its dealings with clients and community groups with whom we worked 'in partnership' had, or so it seemed, caved in overnight.

Social workers are at risk of assault by their clients, and there is evidence to suggest that this risk has increased in recent years in England. Child protection work in any country, at any time, will give rise to powerful feelings of anxiety in practitioners because of the intense and primitive quality of the feelings and identifications involved in contact with abused children and abusing adults (Cooper 1992, Hadjisky 1987). Equally, attacking social workers, particularly verbally, has become something of a national pastime in England in the last decade, and the source of this opprobrium has more than anything else been their perceived professional failure in the realm of child protection work. Protective screens are an all too obvious metaphor for the way social workers feel about themselves in the 1990s, and for how they believe they are seen by the public. Yet in an aptly titled report on the findings of a national opinion poll, *Yourselves as others see you* (*Community Care*, 1987), social workers were ranked below doctors, police officers, teachers and nurses in their importance to the community, but paradoxically their 'advice' was highly valued. As one commentator remarks,

"The evidence, uncertain as it is, is far from totally damning. Social workers remain convinced, however, that they have a negative public image." (Wroe, 1988, p.4)

Whatever the reality of public attitudes, it is now a commonplace observation that professional child protection practices have been profoundly influenced by the *perceived* climate of public hostility towards social work. The so-called 'checklist culture' of child protection work, the reliance on spurious indicators of objectivity in risk assessment and so on, is widely seen within the profession as evidence of defensive practice. The true function of these methodologies is not to protect children better, nor even really to protect social workers from making mistakes, but to protect social workers from the *fear* of making mistakes. And yet, the methodologies themselves have professional and social effects which are all too real.

In her classic paper, Menzies Lyth (1960) described how the social structure and ordering of a hospital was profoundly shaped by the need for nursing staff to defend themselves against the day to day anxieties of working with death, loss, illness and intimate contact with patients' bodies. Defences against anxiety had become institutionalised, a powerful force shaping collective professional behaviour and relationships. Our work in France and

England has led us to believe that the influences on the degree of professional anxiety experienced by practitioners are complex. Anxiety flows from the nature of the 'primary task' of child protection work but it is clear that structural and cultural features of particular child protection systems can either contain or exacerbate these anxieties. Preston-Shoot and Agass (1990,) have described very well the operation of a number of 'vicious circles' or 'games without end' which characterise the inter-relationship of English child protection work and the wider society. Professional anxiety and defensiveness leads to social work assuming the role of social scapegoat, forever trying harder to do better, thereby internalising and accommodating to unrealistic social expectations. When failure occurs, as it inevitably will, the profession has all but created itself as a soft target, and can only respond by agreeing to learn the law better, punish a little more, understand a little less, intervene both more frequently and less, and try harder next time. In the remainder of this chapter, we endeavour to show not just that this state of affairs does not pertain everywhere, but also why it pertains in England, and the particular historical and social conditions which have facilitated its emergence.

The social dynamics of accusation

"They must have children who die", said a mystified English practitioner on first contact with French social work. "Maybe they blame the parents, not social workers." This worker's reaction is notable for at least two reasons. First, her assumption that social workers everywhere are blamed for 'child protection failures' in the way that they are in England, but also her implicit belief that *somebody* is going to be blamed. There is little doubt that the case dynamics of child protection work in France exhibit underlying patterns of accusation and blame which are familiar and recognisable to English practitioners. A recent French feature film, *A Shadow of Doubt (L'Ombre du Doute*, Isserman, 1993) tells the story of an 11-year-old girl who alleges sexual abuse against her father. He denies it and her mother does not believe her. Nevertheless, he is charged, put on remand with an injunction to live away from the family which he breaks, and is jailed. The girl's *éducatrice* meets with a hostile reception from the parents ("Do you have children yourself...?"), but persists in her belief in the child's story, particularly after she runs away from home in the company of her four-year-old brother. The girl's schoolfriends ostracise her. The *éducatrice* and the Children's Judge are shown sharing a glass of whisky together in the judge's office, and planning how to obtain an admission from the father. The judge orders family therapy and some family secrets emerge, but no confession. Finally, the story turns on the breakdown of mother's denial in the face of questioning about an incident in which she saw her husband emerging from her daughter's room in the middle of the night. We are shown father experiencing flashbacks to his own history of childhood abuse. The child's friends reconcile themselves to her, ashamed of their unthinking rejection. The case comes to trial, and although there is no 'hard evidence' the child's lawyer is optimistic – "Believing children changes the world!" Father is convicted, jailed, and is shown confessing and acknowledging his own childhood history.

Despite its title, the film eschews exploration of subtler questions of truth, memory, and reality – the ambiguity of the 'real event' (Scott, 1988). What it does portray is how the dynamics of accusation, denial and the search for truth, inexorably draw the actors in these living dramas into occupying polarised and tightly scripted roles. Whether or not we think there *are* absolute perpetrators and absolute victims in child abuse cases, and whether or not we believe in a single uncontaminated 'truth' about 'what happened', the dynamic pull towards enacting a script which offers only these parts and these endings is powerful and pervasive. In this sense, *A Shadow of Doubt*, offers a faithful narrative, but not a questioning one.

Lorraine Fox Harding (1991) observes that child care and protection debates are an unusual area of social policy where it is very difficult to remain neutral because of the emotional processes involved.

> "...as indicated, the perception of child care issues is sharpened emotionally by the fact that everyone has been a child and most people have had one (or would like to have one). In the contemplation of particular problems and disputes, it appears that onlookers may identify with just one party in the dispute... It is suggested that the majority of media reports of severe child abuse cases in Britain both reflect and encourage an identification with the child, who is portrayed entirely as a victim, while little or no identification is made with the abusing parent. Alternatively in some – though probably fewer – cases, the story is implicitly or explicitly presented entirely from the (supposedly innocent) parents' point of view, encouraging identification with them." (1991, p.7)

English social workers need no introduction to the question of their bad treatment by the popular media, although as Wroe

(1988) and Aldridge (1990) point out, the reality is more complex than most of us in the profession assume, and we should be sceptical of any simple model of direct and unidirectional influence of public opinion by the news media. What does deserve further analysis is how and why the British media have almost without exception become actors in the public drama of child abuse, rather than commentators upon it. This phenomenon is unknown in France and a source of some astonishment to French observers:

> "Stressful. That is really the way social work seems to be in Great Britain. I asked my English colleagues to give me some front pages of recent national newspapers, and what I read was a big surprise:
>
> 'Sack the lot and start again' (Daily Mail)
> 'Social workers must look for fact not fantasy' (The Guardian)
> 'Social work prowess called into question' (The Guardian)
>
> "Public attitudes like these are a big surprise for French social workers... By comparison, in France, the problem of child abuse appeared for the first time in the pages of national newspapers in 1985, when the Ministry of Social Affairs initiated a national campaign for the prevention of maltreatment, and in 1987 with another one about sexual abuse." (Grevot 1994, p.39)

It is one of the ironies of English public life, that in a culture which supposedly defends the family as a haven of privacy, it is the misfortune of certain families that their innermost secrets and pain should become the raw material of mass voyeurism, contempt and vilification. When abusing parents are paraded on the front pages as 'monsters', and social workers as 'wimps', 'bullies', or 'Gestapo', they are being constructed as the essential representational counterparts to the 'innocent' child or parental 'victims' of which Fox Harding writes. Just as the dynamics of direct work with families turn on the question of identifications, so also in the news media.

> " 'Human interest' is the great grabber of consumer attention, and one of its main vehicles is identification. Here, too, social work is in difficulties... Any identification is reserved for the innocent, as in deaths through child abuse. In such cases, the social worker seems to be associated with the accused. Death has the advantage of being unambiguous, producing both victim and villain." (Aldridge, 1990 p.616)

Accused and accuser, innocent and guilty, hero and villain,

oppressor and victim – the precise representation may change, the fairy tale remains the same. But if, as we suggest above, these do tend to be the characteristic dynamics of child protection practice in France as well as England, how is it that in the former they are not re-enacted in the societal arena? Public issues may sometimes mirror the dynamics of private troubles, but not always or inevitably.

The social structuring of anxiety

As we have seen, faced with the same case study of a family in which there are gradually escalating child protection concerns but no clear 'evidence', the English child protection workers who carry statutory responsibility in their daily work became anxious and felt immobilised much more quickly than their French counterparts (Cooper et al, 1992). In terms of immediate practice realities, there were several reasons for this.

First, as we have already seen, English workers believed (correctly) that they could not consider the use of statutory intervention unless they had legally admissible evidence with which to support a case. Faced with unco-operative parents, they were helpless to act. By contrast, their French colleagues were able to make use of parental resistance as a *reason* to bring the case before the Children's Judge. Second, because English social workers are obliged to operate within the legal discourse of individual rights, they were acutely aware of their responsibility not to infringe or neglect anyone's rights. Aware of their primary task, the duty to protect the child, they were also aware of a secondary responsibility, to protect and respect the rights of parents. But these responsibilities were in tension, and not surprisingly the group began to argue among themselves, enacting through identification the competing interests of the two main parties. The argument tended to centre on whether or not there was enough evidence to justify bringing a case to court, but a subsidiary struggle also emerged between workers mainly pre-occupied with establishing the evidence question and those trying to think about the needs of the child and other family members. At times, the latter appeared to be heard by the former as trying to manipulate the legal debate through appeal to sentiment, and were pointed back to consider the quality and quantity of evidence. Periodically, like a slow drumbeat, the voice of one member of the group, a team leader, could be heard – "Our primary responsibility is to protect the child".

The components of the professional anxiety in this scene are several. These workers feel that they carry responsibility for the welfare of the child, but do not have the power to discharge their responsibility. They are barred by the rules of evidence from access to the legal arena which could grant them the control they feel they need, and they are barred by the parents from access to the family which could grant them the reassurance they need. Invested primarily, but not only, with a duty to protect the child, they are *conflicted about their relationship to the family as a whole*, parents and children, whose separate rights *and* needs they must consider, but cannot. In her comparative study of French and English child protection workers, Barre (1993) found that "the conflict most often mentioned by English social workers was between the needs of the child as against those of the family" And as this participant suggests, the social worker is in addition likely to be the focus of equivalent anxieties stemming from other involved agencies:

> "I think there's this worry about what is actually going on in the home, when nobody's telling us and we haven't got any proper evidence, particularly as the family are resistant to our help. It's very difficult when we haven't actually got the evidence to remove the children. I think there would be a lot of pressures on us from other agencies to remove them, possibly."

The source of anxiety in this, very familiar, situation is a blockage, in particular to the possibility of resolving conflict. The block is across the entrance to the seat of power, the courts. But the courts, as much as social services, are a part of the child protection system, and it is the structural disconnection of these two spheres of the system which is a principle source of the anxiety experienced by English child protection workers. These practitioners are professionally and personally vulnerable in two mutually reinforcing ways. First to the fear that they will fail in their responsibilities to children and parents, and second that they will be attacked for these failures. The further irony in this situation is that one likely source of public criticism is judges themselves, the senior representatives of the very sphere of the child protection system within which social workers *need* to function in a proper partnership. The anxiety is, as one practitioner expressed it, of "being slapped by the hand that does not feed you".

In their discussion of the emotional and systemic roots of inter-professional dysfunction in social work, Will and Baird (1984) note that there are at least three contributory sources to conflicts among professional groups trying to collaborate on cases. First, personal characteristics of practitioners may play their part; second, factors within particular families are likely to contribute to professional discord; and third, "there are real differences between different professions and different agencies which make some inter-professional relationships more vulnerable than others to trouble and conflict." (1984) These factors may coalesce to produce powerful processes of splitting among professionals, and mirroring of family dynamics by workers. As they suggest, the particular nature of inter-professional differences or tensions may offer "lines of least resistance", along which these dynamics may be enacted. In the appendix to their important study of anxiety and inter-professional collaboration, Woodhouse and Pengelly (1991) offer a compelling analysis of the Cleveland affair noting, amongst many other factors, the way in which professional blame centred on women in positions of responsibility in the various agencies so that it was "as if the service network was re-enacting not only the abuse of female by male, but also the disastrous failure of co-parenting by male *and* female which child sexual abuse in the family represents" (1991).

At the widest level of the organisation of the English child protection system, it is our contention that the particular form of the relationship between the law and social work represents a 'line of least resistance' along which many of our systems' troubles flow and proliferate, allowing the dynamics of 'private troubles' to emerge, mirrored and magnified, as 'public issues'. The partition of power and responsibility for child protection work between the courts and social work leaves social workers carrying an un-reasonable burden of professional anxiety, a kind of 'double dose' arising both from worrying about children in their care, and about themselves. When something does 'go wrong', the power invested in the judiciary combines with the adversarial and rights-based character of the system of justice, to facilitate a re-enactment of a basic dynamic of child protection work – abuse and accusation of abuse – in the public arena of the court, the public enquiry and finally the media. Only at this level, it is social workers who become the subjects of accusation and abuse. The courts and their representatives may quite fairly disclaim any responsibility because apart from discharging their function of hearing evidence and making a disposal, they are not asked to carry responsibility. However, insofar as the judiciary has the power to apportion it to others, we should note that the concept of 'responsibility' in adversarial systems of justice is specific, reflecting ideologies of 'legal positivism' in which 'legal facts' are gathered, analysed, and yield up a verdict on individual behaviour in terms of a restricted binary code – guilty or innocent. (King and Piper, 1991) It is small wonder then, that as Aldridge (1990) notes, sometimes the most 'responsible' of our media organs can end by humming this tune to its readers, for "Even *The Guardian* has admitted slapping an inappropriate 'The Social Worker Dunnit' headline on a story".

We do not intend the above analysis to be read deterministically. Mica Nava (1988) has analysed media coverage of the Cleveland affair with attention to the scapegoating of Marietta Higgs and the media construction of a gallery of specifically female rogues. Among child abuse 'scandals' Cleveland was unusual for the complexity of the issues it raised, for how it undermined previously reliable moral and conceptual schemata, so that "in many newspapers, the uncertainty that this lack of closure has produced has been manifest in the contradictory messages conveyed in different articles on the same page, and even within articles..." (1988). Despite this lack of ideological closure, Nava traces how the "chains of association and processes of displacement" were formed which demonised the woman paediatrician rather than her male colleague, and as she became linked with feminism, metropolitan socialism, and homosexuality, in this way "the spectre of feminism becomes folk devil". Social work and social work practitioners did not escape in Cleveland and the discourses which ensnared them partly overlap with those uncovered by Nava. But whoever occupies the role of folk devil in these dramas, it is clear that such moral panics are highly structured events, the structures being associative and mythological as well as organisational, but in neither case rational. Hall *et al* (1978) argued the case for a different kind of structuring of such events, and pointed to the way in which moral panics facilitate increased state intervention, often of a coercive kind. In the recent English history of child abuse, this appears to have been the case. Nigel Parton (1991) has shown how the impetus during the 1980s towards a more consensual and 'partnership-oriented' child protection system came into tension with the moral and political climate generated by the succession of child death enquiries in the last years of the decade. Of these two "competing agendas or paradigms for practice" (1991 p.78) it was the legalistic one represented by the public enquiry which largely won out. In the Children Act it is as though they survive in an unwilling and unequal cohabitation, and one question which the present book seeks to address is 'How might they be enabled to meet on better terms?'

The social dynamics of containment

After watching a video recording of a group of French *éducateurs*
discussing the same case study, one of the group of English child
protection workers described above said:

> "They made a distinction between pressure and negotiation,
> most of them, saying that though people might have different
> views, they would negotiate and come to some decision
> between them, and they seemed sure that would happen, that it
> was something which could be resolved."

Much of this confidence that in French child protection cases
'things can be resolved' stems from the partnership which
éducateurs have with the Children's Judge, and the assumption
that a triangular collaboration can be established with the family.
The relationship between the two key professionals is not one of
equals. Partnership does not mean equality, but reciprocity of
role, commitment and professional understanding. The job of the
Children's Judge is a fairly low status one in the hierarchy of the
French judiciary and some stay with it only a short while before
advancing their careers, while others take it as a vocation. The
judges are trained at the *École Nationale de la Magistrature* at
Bordeaux, but their role is unlike that of other magistrates and
judges in the French system, reflecting their participation in a
system designed "to interpret and deal with child protection issues
as essentially family problems" (King and Trowell, 1992).

The social work-legal partnership of the Children's Judge and
éducateurs has both a formal and an informal dimension. Social
workers operate under the legal authority and direction of the
judge, but with autonomy over their day to day professional
decisions and interventions. Any important changes in a case plan
(such as a change of placement) must be agreed by the judge, and
where there is an order in force it must be formally reviewed by
the judge every six months. Judges do not manage the social work
services supporting them, but do effectively direct the overall work
of *éducateurs* (Ely and Stanley, 1990). Since they are ultimately
accountable for the cases under their direction, judges carry both
power and formal responsibility with respect to child protection
work.

This does not mean that French social workers are reduced to
humble under-labourers or mere technicians in the service of a
managing director, or that they feel powerless in their work. In
fact, as we shall see, the opposite is nearer the truth; the
intermeshing of the welfare and justice dimensions of the total
child protection task results in judges and social workers each

assuming considerable professional responsibility for both aspects. Jacques Bourquin (1994) has described the evolution of the role of the Children's Judge since 1945, introducing an emphasis on prevention as they realised that their interventions were often 'too little, too late' (JCLT, 1994). This led to judges becoming involved in the setting up of residential provision for young people, and in the 1950s the idea of the *'juge éducateur'* ('judge-social worker') was commonplace. In the 1970s many judges were trained in systemic thinking in the social sciences which led to the notion of the 'therapeutic judge'. A recent text by a Children's Judge gives a flavour of current practice:

> "How does the judge assess the likely danger to a child? We have seen that we are dealing with a dual perspective, the judge's and that of the specialists. The medical, social and psychological assessments have a different, but equal legitimacy to that of the judge's. The two are interactive, and the issue should be tackled according to a dynamic model." (Badouin, 1990, p.78)

Baudouin continues with a sophisticated discussion of the delicate balance judges must strike between implementing the law and obtaining the co-operation of reluctant parents and children, of the problems of managing the fluid boundary between his role and those of the welfare services, and of the strategic, even therapeutic, use of his authority with families. In the end, says Badouin, the best guarantee for both children and parents, and of the effective implementation of a statutory order, "rests with the judge's competence, and his ability to make good use of the competence of his partners – doctors, psychologists, social workers and so on" (1990).

Professional attitudes like these are not simply a matter of a different 'legal culture' prevailing in France, although there is no doubt that the traditions of Roman Law and an inquisitorial system of justice may lend themselves to a more integrated and family-oriented approach to statutory child care (King and Trowell, 1992). Rather, they derive from the existence of a structured inter-relationship between the domains of law and welfare in the French child protection system. We have already noted the 'annexation' of the discourses of child welfare by the discourses of law in the last decade in English child protection work. But this process, amply confirmed by our own comparative analyses of the preoccupations of English and French prac- titioners in relation to identical case material, could not have taken place unless social work was vulnerable to this kind of 'colonisation' (Cooper et al, 1992). It is because the law and social work in England do not form a structured inter-dependent totality, with the ensuing reciprocal professional investment by actors in different spheres of the system, that one component institution can easily come to dominate another.

Barre's (1993) comparative study confirms a number of themes identified in our own research. She found that the division of labour or 'discontinuity' in French child protection work wherein the investigative function and the responsibility for surveillance under statutory order are clearly separated, contrasted with the continuity of function of the English local authority child protection worker who may see a case through from referral to adoption. Unsurprisingly, English social workers commented that in the transition from a 'helping' to a 'controlling' role, families become "less disposed to be open and more hostile", and that it is in the process of gathering evidence that the seeds of conflict between social workers and families are sown (1991). English practitioners effectively fulfil the judicial role of the French *Procureur de la République* who is responsible for evaluating whether cases should come before the court. In our earlier study (Cooper et al, 1992), we found that the discourse of French child protection workers revolved around the concepts of the 'suffering' of the child, and the need to gather 'information' in order that they and the judge could reach an 'understanding' of the family situation. The equivalent discursive spaces in England were occupied by the concepts of the implicit or explicit 'guilt or innocence' of the abusers, and the requirement to obtain 'evidence' in order to furnish a 'proof'. When asked about the role of 'proof' and 'evidence' in their work, French workers in Barre's study replied variously that its collection was "not part of the social work function", that it "would render the role no longer one of giving help, but of social control" and, pertinently, that "it is not necessary to gather proof in order to identify a child's suffering" (1991). Insofar as conflict is a primary cause of professional anxiety Barre's conclusions are significant – that both French and English workers' roles do entail contradictory relationships with families, but that the intensity of this is significantly less in France than in England.

What then of the French social worker's relationship to 'law' when compared with that of their English counterparts? Paradoxically, *éducateurs* were consistently impressed by English workers' detailed knowledge of legislation, and went home resolved to do better in this respect themselves. Of course, this is less of a paradox than it at first sight appears. Not only is the legal basis of French child protection work somewhat simpler than that of England, but the successful prosecution of the child protection task in England depends on substantial knowledge of due legal process. However, the more meaningful comparison concerns social workers' relationships with their own authority with respect to their work. English practitioners implementing a statutory order may feel that they bear the authority of the court, but this is not necessarily translated into a secure internal sense of their *own power*. As we have seen, there is good reason for social workers to feel ambivalent about the power of the judiciary to affect their professional behaviour. Compare this with Patrick Regnault's description of his work as an *éducateur*:

"There was a case, a boy who hadn't been to school for about six months, so I went round in the morning and found him in bed. I didn't explain myself particularly, I said 'Get up', and left him to decide whether he wanted to negotiate anything with me. In fact, he got up, I drove him to school, and took him to the headteacher where I said 'This is your pupil, you probably have things to say to each other'. It must have had an impact on him because he went to school for the next year. I'm sure that if I was in such a situation here, I couldn't do that. I would be saying 'I am the social worker, under section whatever of the law I have to tell you that...' My feeling is that a lot of social work here is quite wishy-washy in this respect. There was quite a Lacanian influence in social work in France at this time – making people ask questions rather than providing answers... For example, I would have said of this boy, we cannot possibly leave him in his state of omnipotence. There would be an attempt to think about the law at both a social level and also a symbolic, a psychological one." (1994 p.45)

We are reminded in this account of Badouin's view of the relationship between legal, psychological, social and medical influences in assessing risk to children. Regnault distinguishes, but does not disconnect from each other, the social, psychological and legal sources for the authority he carries into the situation. His characterisation of 'wishy-washy' English social workers' attitudes to authority is precisely because this authority is felt to belong *elsewhere*, in an abstract and remote realm called 'the law'. If, as we suggested in Chapter 1, French child protection work is characterised by personalised relationships, rather than the more abstract style associated with a role culture, then this extends to carrying a secure sense of personal authority within the limits of the professional remit. And as we also pointed out in Chapter 1, this does not inevitably lead to the capricious or arbitrary functioning of the system. As Regnault goes on to say:

> "In social work in France, if you don't get your point across in front of the judge, then you can always put it across somewhere else... I found it very safe in France, that whatever I was doing would be looked at by other people, that I was not all powerful. It was important to know there were parts of the judicial system working in favour of the people whose lives I barged into." (1994, p.46)

This is a way of saying that he felt *protected*. Protected from the possibility, or the temptation, or the fear that he might act destructively towards those people over whom he had power. Feeling protected enabled him to carry authority with confidence. Among the figures who act as protectors is the Children's Judge. Now, this state of affairs stands in marked contrast to the experience of English practitioners, who rarely, if ever, experience the courts in this way. Rather, as we have seen, going to court is a feared event, a 'trial'.

And yet, we observed a curious paradox in the responses of English practitioners as they came to understand the workings of the French system and the role of the Children's Judge. Noting that the powers of the judge did not seem to be formally circumscribed, that she or he could implement orders without hearing evidence, practitioners both welcomed the ease of access this afforded to the legal arena, but also expressed anxiety about the absence of clear rules for determining the presence or absence of abuse. In some respects these concerns related to the apparent absence of mechanisms for guaranteeing rights. But it also seemed that English practitioners *relied for their own protection* on the process of determining cases through evaluation of legal evidence. In dispute with a colleague about the status of the available 'evidence' in a case study example, an English practitioner said, "You just... you shouldn't be destroying families without evidence." The actions of English practitioners in child protection cases can and do lead to the 'destruction' of families through the permanent separation of children from parents, in a way that is much rarer and more difficult to effect in France. Quite understandably, English workers need to feel supported and legitimated in this task, at a professional, social and political level. But the contradictions in this state of affairs are acute, for the very same rules of evidence which at times deny workers the power to act on their legitimate anxieties about children at risk, must at others be invoked by them as a form of protection against the psychic anxiety involved in 'destroying families'. Needing help with this onerous task, English social workers find themselves working in the shadow of a legal system which, clear rules of evidence notwithstanding, might reasonably be described as arbitrary and capricious in its overall functioning, and not the consistent, benign, and protective authority which they deserve. For English workers, it may be very hard to experience power as positive and helpful, because too often their use of it is in danger of being condemned as in some way destructive.

The experience of parents and children in the French and English child protection systems is the subject of a detailed study by some of the authors of this book at the time of going to press. However, we opened the first chapter of the present book with an account by an English practitioner of a French family whose children had been the subject of statutory orders. In the same way that French child protection work follows familiar patterns, so the anxieties and tensions experienced by French parents and children are not new to English observers either. But, just as the structure and culture of the French system leads to the *containment* of professional anxiety for *éducateurs*, the same factors contain tension and conflict for families. In part, as we have seen, this is a consequence of the genuinely informal atmosphere which pervades the conduct of hearings by the Children's Judge. As one English practitioner said:

> "We witnessed an *audience* with the Children's Judge, and I was most impressed with the way that she talked to the children and also the foster carers and the social worker; the way that the social worker could present a report, but also talked to the judge beforehand and made recommendations."

These perceptions are echoed by Patrick Regnault:

> "One of the main differences I'm struck by is the way kids are treated in court. In France the judge will talk to the child, ask questions – 'Why did you do this?', 'Am I going to see you again?' and the child has to say something. There is a direct appeal to personal responsibility – the judge has said his or her piece and now it's the child's turn." (1994, pp.45-6)

In their study of delinquency prevention and the child protection system in Dunkirk, Ely and Stanley (1990) point to the sense of ownership which French parents and young people seem to have with respect to the court, and also hint at the wider structural explanation of this experience.

> "A contrast which is more difficult to convey is that the French

juveniles and parents seem to act as though the *audience* and the judge belong to them in some way; as if they are all interrelated parts of the same thing. They seem to lack our sense of social distancing and of social exclusion. This reflects not just a particular judge's approach, but French history and social perspectives." (1990, p.14)

This assumption of ownership of the means of legal production gives the lie to the idea that the French child protection system does not validate the rights of individuals. In demonstrating that they feel the court 'in some way belongs to them', ordinary French people are *living* their rights, rather than as in England 'laying claim to them' as something external which must be grasped in case they are witheld or stolen. It is true that in France, unlike in England, one cannot get access to a public statement of the detailed mechanisms by which the rights of individual 'consumers' will be guaranteed, because such manuals do not exist. But after a year of contact with the French way of doing things, many English practitioners in our study had come round to the view that the French system offered a better guarantee of *substantive* rights than did our own, which in turn offers a clearer and more comprehensive guarantee of *formal* rights. But formal rights must be supported by the resources and power to exercise them if they are to be meaningful. It is now required practice that parents attend the whole of child protection case conferences. Yet this still does not happen in some authorities, and where it does most social workers would agree that parents do not feel they are able to use the opportunity to their own benefit. It is hard to imagine an English parent feeling that they 'own' a case conference.

There may be less direct violence in the week to week experience of the French child protection worker, but there is not necessarily less tension and conflict – between professionals, between workers and families and in the families themselves. What seems clear is that the structure of the system contains and manages tensions rather than exacerbating them, partly because the 'caring' and the 'controlling' functions are integrated through the mutually reinforcing roles and responsibilities of judges and social workers, and partly because there is genuine access by all parties to the seat of power. This structure has allowed a very different culture of relationships to flourish among all parties to child protection proceedings than we find in England.

An inverse law?

We have examined a range of inter-related factors which might explain why French child care practitioners seem to experience less professional anxiety about their task than their English counterparts. However, it will be clear that much rests on the figure of the *Juge d'Enfants* in France, and it is reasonable to wonder whether professional anxiety is, at least to some extent, differently distributed in the French system rather than simply better contained. There is some evidence that this is the case, and it is worth setting down the account of one English practitioner who met and talked with a judge:

"He talked to me in great detail about the stresses and strains of the job and he struck me as quite a 'beaten up' person! He said that he felt social workers have it a lot easier than he does, the judge gets all the stick in cases. Social workers have each other, but judges are on their own and have to make decisions on their own, OK with help, but often there's a family that's difficult. You're in that room and you have to make the decision and that's what he found most difficult about the job. He had quite a pained look on his face when he talked about difficult families, who don't appreciate what he's trying to do. And he's been hit, his colleague has been hit, and they've had to take time off work to cope with this. I asked him how he ended up being a judge, and he said, out of interest, he was a customs officer before. There is some status in it, he does get quite a lot of respect for being a Children's Judge, but the job itself is very difficult. The criticism comes from all angles – social workers for example come to him and ask him to do things and most of the time he does what they ask, but sometimes not, because he doesn't think it's the right thing, and he ends up getting a lot of stick. Social workers are thus his primary allies but also his primary enemy, and he was making jovial comments about that with my French colleague, and she was joking back with him. I suppose it's a bit like Social Services and the Voluntary Sector – you're friends but you're also enemies! And the only place he felt support from was outside the profession. There was no 'Oh we're going to meet for counselling now'.

In comparison with English roles, I saw him in part a bit like an Area Manager, but also it was as though he had nowhere to go. If you think about the case conference, then although the chair has to take the decisions, everyone is in the room. With the judge, all the information and assessments have been given to him, but the people are outside the room and the information is in paper form. I think the fact that he is alone must contribute to the pressures of decision-making, and he seemed to agree with that.

But when I attended an *audience* with the same judge, I felt he really did engage with the parents, and then he behaved, in my opinion, like a sort of extended member of the family. 'What are you going to do with yourself, what are you interested in, what do you want to do?' and he put these dilemmas very firmly to this young person, who said 'Well, I don't really know...' and the judge said he was thinking of a particular placement for a period, and they all agreed and everyone signed the forms and it was a kind of participatory process. It was useful although it might have been difficult for the boy, there was no-one there to represent him, if you like!"

One of the striking features of this account is the impression that the dynamics of English relationships between social workers and the judiciary are inverted in France. It is the judge who feels that he 'cannot get it right', that social workers are the ambivalent partners in the joint enterprise, that he is the one who is criticised from all angles, and the recipient of physical violence. Perhaps the 'buck has to stop' somewhere in all child protection systems, although there is some evidence that in Italy where the *Guidice Tutelare* is the equivalent of the Children's Judge, this figure has the support of a panel of judges with which cases are discussed and evaluated.

We should also note that the stresses on the Children's Judge in France may rebound on social workers. A Parisian psychologist, working to the office of the Children's Judge in an assessment team, reports that judges may carry up to a thousand cases in inner city areas. This means that they do not have the ability to follow the progress of cases in depth, build proper relationships with families, and inevitably partnership with social workers can deteriorate into a more managerial relationship in which *éducateurs* find themselves receiving instructions rather than negotiating through dialogue. This psychologist also observes that the occupation of Children's Judge is becoming increasingly 'feminised', a trend she associates with the relatively low status of the judge in the overall judicial hierarchy (Private communication from Mme. Miriam Eyheramandy).

It is possible that the profession of Children's Judge suffers from some of the same structural difficulties which affect child protection work in England. The image of the 'battered judge' resonates with that of the battered social worker. In both cases, although to different degrees, there are problems of professional legitimation, inadequate resources, and structural isolation in a role occupied by individuals who may be torn to shreds by conflicting social, professional and public demands. Nevertheless, as we have seen both the Children's Judge and child protection workers in France are legitimated in their authority, and protected from the worst excesses of ambivalent public reactions to tragedy, through their connection to those with whom they may enter into conflict. In France there is an assumption that it is better to belong to an imperfect society than to be disconnected or cast out from society altogether, and this assumption is translated into a sense of the right of the powerless to insist on being heard, to protest about injustice, to occupy and use the 'space' available for dialogue and struggle. Thus, the structure of the French child protection system embodies the wider commitment to *'inclusion'*, the effort to combat social and individual marginalisation. In England, by contrast, child abuse tragedies become the vehicle through which from time to time we may cast our own demons into outer darkness.

Chapter 10: A Tale of Two Cultures: Race Ethnicity and Identity in France and England

After a year of contact with the French child protection system one English practitioner summed up his thoughts thus:

> "I enjoyed the experience very much... but I wonder about the whole idea of 'comparing' things. I think I learned that the social and cultural context makes everything different. At the start of the visits we would talk among ourselves and say 'Oh, we do this better' but in the end you realised that you were just *looking* at something, at the *Frenchness* of it."

For their part, French practitioners underwent a similar process of coming to terms with an experience of irreducible difference. Any reader of the preceding chapters may have already shared in this experience to some extent, and come to appreciate that in both England and France everything seems to be connected to everything else in a way which means it is hard to compare directly isolated practices or attitudes in the two countries. To study a child protection system is, unavoidably, to study a society and to enter the complex interwoven tissue of history, tradition, politics and ideology which goes to make up culture. Any particular aspect of this culture, including child protection practices and institutions, may be looked at in its own right but cannot be fully understood without examining its connections to other practices and ideologies. Child protection work will reflect wider cultural assumptions, but will also contribute to their reproduction and to their evolution and change over time. French and English child protection practices and the systems in which they are located may or may not be internally consistent, but they will 'make sense' in terms of the wider national history and culture. For this reason, the study of another country's social work must be approached in what is best described as an 'anthropological' spirit, and while we want to learn from how the French go about their work, we should be wary of the temptation to beg, steal or borrow the best of their practices without thought to how they can be integrated with our own (Cooper 1992, Cooper and Pitts 1994).

In this chapter we explore how various aspects of French and English child protection work are embedded in the respective political and professional cultures of the two nations. In coming years British social work will have a greater degree of 'cultural exchange' with continental Europe. Many of the characteristic differences between French and English professional and political culture can be generalised to the rest of the continent. In short 'they' often have much more in common with one another than we do with any of 'them'. No doubt this has much to do with barriers of language, and the history of the 'special relationship' with the USA, but it means that the process of exchange, and change, may be peculiarly difficult for English practitioners and policy makers. Nevertheless, the work out of which this book is written did contribute to a process of change as well as increased under- standing although, as we noted at the end of Chapter 7, opportunities to change were more readily available to French practitioners than their English counterparts.

Inclusion and the politics of marginality

In chapter 8 we discussed the evolution of family policy in France and England and related these developments to differing political traditions in the two countries. To understand some of the differences in social work ideology in England and France, for example the markedly contrasting approaches to questions of racial identity in child care work, it is necessary to re-visit these separate histories from a new angle. Dyson (1980) locates France within a 'continental' tradition in which the state is both the sum of its parts and more than the sum.

> "To talk of the state is not to list its institutions; the state represents the spirit of the community and is the site of all legitimate power (In the Anglo-American tradition) the state can only be thought of as a list of all the components of institutional authority, legitimate power being dispersed among

the centre, regional bodies and groups."

We have seen in earlier chapters how the French do not conceive of the family, or particular families, as outside the state but as integral to it. When family members claim their 'right' to belong to the state, to participate in its structures and argue about their grievances, in the office of the Children's Judge, for example, they are exercising their citizenship, the contract which says that they belong to the French nation state and it belongs to them – '*La France, c'est moi*'. As Walter Lorenz observes:

> "This means that the powers of the state in the continental concept are on the one hand more visible and manifest, and on the other hand they are more explicitly prescribed, and in principle subjected to the scrutiny of the 'citizen'... It controls them, haunts them at times with the spectre of the police state, but is to an extent also controlled by them." (1994, p.17)

The nature of this contract can be best understood by looking at what happens in France when it is perceived to be failing. French society in the 1990s is no less vulnerable than England to the effects of recession, unemployment and housing difficulties. But the tradition of an overarching responsibility of the state for its citizens means that the effects of these social forces on people's lives is necessarily a matter of state concern. At both a micro and a macro social level unemployment is not conceived of as a discrete social or economic problem, but as part of a matrix of forces which contribute to social *exclusion*. '*Exclusion*' is in fact a very inclusive concept, rather like that of 'the underclass' which for a time hovered on the edges of respectable British political discourse, but never quite crystallised. Often it is mentioned in the same breath as 'poverty', at others with 'unemployment'. A common assertion is that its three vital elements are unemployment, health and housing, and nearly as often that it denotes marginalisation in economic, social and cultural terms. But there is an important thread of argument which links '*inclusion*' with the idea of 'citizenship', the capacity not just to have a job or a home, but to participate in and contribute to political processes and social reproduction. A recent analysis of *exclusion* in the journal *L'Événements* (1994) includes statistics for illiteracy, psychiatric and penal populations, homelessness, the long term unemployed, and the beneficiaries of RMI, which since 1988 has been the French government's major policy initiative to combat *exclusion*, offering participants a guaranteed minimum income in return for their involvement in training, employment and educational programmes.

What is noticeable from an English perspective is that the categories of 'race', 'gender', or 'sexuality' do not figure prominently in this discourse, except insofar as they are required to identify important sub-sets or trends within the overall focus on social marginality. Thus 'single mothers' are recognised as a significantly large group within social security claimants, and the figures for illiteracy refer to a high proportion of north African people. There is no assumption that social identity refers primarily to an aspect of individual identity such as ethnicity, skin colour, sex, sexuality, or any aggregation of these. Such identity referents *may* assume prominence under given socio-economic or cultural conditions, but this would be understood to point to a local and/or temporary failure of the fundamental project of the nation-state which is the *'inclusion'* or social connection within the state of all citizens irrespective of individual identity.

Universality, pluralism and the politics of identity

Robert Miles argues that while the French, Dutch and British states all claim that they are pursuing a policy of 'integration' with respect to ethnic minority or 'immigrant' groups, the concept of 'integration' is nationally variable in the sense that:

> "...within Europe, what it means to 'belong' varies from one nation state to another...French researchers often distinguish between the French 'way of doing things' and the 'Anglo-Saxon tradition'. Behind this dichotomy lies a conception of the distinctiveness of the French nation state which is seen to originate in the French revolution...a distinctiveness which is expressed in the contemporary nature of the mode of affinity to the French nation...This distinction is structured by universalism, by the notion of the French nation as the expression of the collectivity of equal and active citizens, a structuring that is thought to be absent in Britain and the Netherlands, which are characterised alternatively (and in polar opposition) as social formations shaped by institutional pluralism and decentralisation." (1993, p.176)

The tensions between these different conceptions of the relationship between the state and minority groupings were clearly expressed by French and English social workers in their dealings with each other. As one French worker said, "In France, if there is an ideology it is one of citizenship and an integrationist mentality." This was echoed, but with qualifications, by an English worker who noted that 'black' French people wanted to see themselves as first and foremost 'French', and secondarily as 'black'.

> "There is just 'the family', irrespective of culture and difference, it's a basic assumption. There is the notion of the universal family, and of citizenship, both of which are very strong...but these hide differences in France, and in England in the last 15 or 20 years it's been about saying, 'Let's grapple with this' ".

It was noticeable that the conceptualisations of French practitioners with respect to the politics of race in their child protection work seemed consistent with that of wider French ideology, commentary and analysis about this issue. This is by no means the case with English workers, whose perspectives reflected the dominant discourses of British anti-discriminatory and anti-oppressive social work practice faithfully enough, a stance which in turn sets them apart from a whole range of other, semi-official competing discourses about race in British public life. In itself this speaks of what might be called the greater 'vertical cohesion' of French political culture and practice, by comparison with the heterogeneity and pluralism in British political life of which Robert Miles writes.

French practitioners were struck by the consistency and frequency of references to questions of power, oppression, empowerment, anti-discriminatory practice, and the needs of ethnic and other minorities in the discourse of English workers. One French worker commented on the very positive images conveyed publicly with respect to black people, gay people and single parents in the English agency which he visited. However, it was the preoccupation of their English colleagues with questions of race which struck French practitioners most forcibly. They understood policy and practice concerns to be aimed at the preservation of cultural and racial identity, and noted same-race placement policies and organisational efforts to recruit ethnic minority practitioners as expressions of these aims. But, it is no exaggeration to say that they experienced these features of English practice as entirely alien. In one discussion French workers expressed their astonishment at their English counterparts' equally astonished reaction that a non-Jewish child could be placed with a Jewish family in France. Similarly in one English case the imperative to find a foster mother of the same racial origin as the child, occasioned both astonishment and a degree of disturbance. As we saw in Chapter 1, the typical reaction of a French social worker to practices like these, is to see in them the seeds of a segregated society. For English workers, they represent the effort to combat the deleterious consequences of a society already divided and imbued with racism, in which the promotion of a 'positive identity' will be an aid to psychological and social survival.

In her paper about the absence of 'political correctness' in France, Lisa Appignanasi (1994) cites a recent survey of first generation French North African people between the ages of 19 and 30 which showed that over 70% felt closer to the French way of life and French culture than the culture of their parents. She adds that the degree of 'integration' rises with levels of education, and that integration is seen as good by the majority of both Maghrebians, people of North African origin, and French non-Maghrebians – "An American style culture of rigorous ethnic separateness and splintering is seen to lead logically only to apartheid" French social work practitioners reported that Maghrebian families often request that their children be placed with white French families, because they see this as a healthy contribution to *intégration*. It is tempting to respond to information of this kind with a familiar English repertoire of questions and reservations about 'internalised racism' or 'institutionalised racism'. But as Appignanasi points out, no-one is actually arguing that France is any less (or more) 'racist' than Britain:

> "It is simply that the analysis of ethnic questions is different, as is what can be done to ease race relations. In a recent demonstration by SOS Racisme (one of several anti-racism organisations) which targeted the new tougher immigration laws, the placards had an unfamiliar ring. *'Un raciste c'est quelqu'un qui se trompe de colère'* trumpeted some: a racist is someone who has found a mistaken object for his anger, or a racist is someone who's made a mistake about colour – punning on the closeness of sound of *'colère'* and *'coleur'*. Racism, in other words, marks a mistake of analysis. Difference is not the primary cause of social ills..." (1994, p.154)

A common response of English social workers and liberal academics on first encountering the French politics of race is to liken it to the bygone era of British 'multi-culturalism' and assimilationism, and remark that France seems to be 'where we were ten or fifteen years ago'. The unspoken implication here is that 'they'll catch up sooner or later'. But as we suggested at the start of this chapter, we should no more attempt to foist English ways of thinking on the French, than go in search of borrowed solutions to problems we must address for ourselves. The history and trajectories of the politics of race in France are different but this does not mean that exchange or learning cannot occur, or did not occur in the course of interactions between child protection workers from the two countries. A black English practitioner reported that on his second visit to France, and his fourth meeting with his (white) opposite number, she had suggested it might be interesting for him to meet and talk with a black residential worker. "This was the first time I had felt acknowledged as a black person with a particular cultural identity," he commented. Equally, it was clear that for the French worker concerned, the effort to make the arrangement described above represented an act of 'cultural deviation', arrived at after a period of struggle with the threat to the French worker's own assumptions and expectations, embodied in the practices and the person of her English colleague.

The power of these assumptions is articulated by the French sociologist Dominique Schnapper, who distinguishes between those European countries which have tended historically towards an ideal of 'collective integration', of groupings which retain a discrete identity, and those which espouse 'individual integration' into the body politic, thus subsuming any group identity:

> "...in countries like Great Britain and the Netherlands which recognise cultural particularity, and are closer to the ideal of collective integration, the concepts of community or ethnic minority and of race are legitimised as if their definition were self-evident." (1992, p.99)

It is the 'self-evidence' of these categories in the discourse and practice of the English workers which French practitioners found so striking and unsettling, and which in turn English workers reacted to in France, for as Schnapper goes on to say, "A politics which aims at the integration of individuals cannot but be 'colour blind': particular measures, to address needs of ethnic groups, are seen as discriminatory." (1992) In view of the scorn poured upon the politics of 'colour blindness' in left of centre English political thought over the last decade, it is hardly surprising that an encounter with this ideology raised the temperature of Anglo-French interactions. Equally, as Robert Miles points out, for French, Dutch and German governments of the 1980s *intégration* has been posed as part of the solution to racism, while

> "A Race Relations act (of which there have been three in Britain since the mid-1960s) is inconceivable in these three countries because it would be instantly interpreted as legislation intended to regulate relations between different 'races' in a

manner that echoes the 'final solution' to the 'Jewish problem'." (1993, p.20)

Clearly, there is an enormous burden of significance attaching to the ideologies which inform the politics of race in child protection practice in both countries. To what extent then is it possible, or indeed desirable, to offer a critique of either country from the perspective of the other on this matter? We found not only that English practitioners were able, over time, to enter constructive debate with their French colleagues but also that there are signs of recognition from within France of the importance of some of our ways of thinking about anti-racist practice. Additionally, there are signs that some aspects of French ideology are echoed in recent British work which questions the central tenets of 'identity politics' without abandoning a focus on the significance of 'race' in social work and other practices.

In one French child protection case involving a north African family in which a very young child was, at one point, being considered for adoption, the *éducateur* reported that the parents were apparently disengaged and unconcerned about his future. The English practitioner noted that in parallel circumstances the attempt would be made to find a worker of similar ethnic origins, and wondered if the family did not fully understand the significance of what was being proposed for their child – perhaps language difficulties partly accounted for their lack of engagement? In her view there was no consideration of the possibility that culturally different styles of parenting might structure perception of the case. It appeared that questions of this kind could be assimilated by French workers as relevant to and supportive of the more central professional value of 'keeping the family together'.

Val-Fourre' in the town of Mantes-la-Jolie is one of the new Parisian suburbs, a massive concentration of high rise blocks with a huge population of north African people and other families originating from France's former colonies, a site like many other *banlieus* (suburbs) of everything which *exclusion* represents. The mayor of Mantes, who is also president of the local hospital tells the following story. White nurses in the maternity wards had become angry and frustrated with the behaviour of Senegalese women after they had given birth, because their habit was to hand the baby over to nurses to look after while they received a never ending stream of relatives and visitors who brought large quantities of rich (and in the nurses view unsuitable) food into the wards and sat around eating with the new mother. The mothers, for their part, were consistently complaining that "the nurses in that hospital treat us like prostitutes". The mayor undertook his own enquiries and discovered that in the region of Senegal from which these families originate, a new mother is 'a queen for a week' and is fêted, dined and generally fussed over while other people take care of the newborn. The only women to whom this ritual is not extended are prostitutes.

The mayor instigated a training programme for hospital staff to educate them about these cultural particularities, and arranged parallel processes whereby the nurses' past behaviour could be explained to local women. "We have to integrate", says the mayor. "What choice is there?" This is recognisable in terms of what might be called 'culturally sensitive practice' in English social work, and insofar as culturally insensitive practices may constitute one aspect of racist practice, it is anti-racist within the meaning of English ideologies. As Cannan et al. note,

> "The ways in which schools should respond to issues of language, religious teaching and culture (for example girls covering their heads) has become a matter of debate, but the socialist government which came to power in 1981 has promoted the idea of *insertion*: that is, integration into society with a right to difference rather than colonial assimilation and loss of cultural identity. (1992, pp. 39-40)

It is mistaken to assume that 'universalism' is wholly incompatible with a politics of difference or vice versa. While as Miles (1993) points out, the notion of 'integration' assumes that there are groupings who are 'unintegrated', and therefore constructed by definition as 'other' to the host nation, the struggle of racial minorities to achieve citizenship, combat racism, and acquire the right to full participation in society, has different starting points in different countries, is mediated by different languages and histories and takes place along different, continually developing, trajectories.

Writing from an Anglo-American perspective, Paul Gilroy has emerged in Anglophone debate as the most coherent critic of current trends in the politics of race. Gilroy's work stands foursquare with the history of western imperialism and racism, but eschews the over-determined characteristics of much contemporary 'race politics' in which he detects the reappearance of concepts of 'ethnic absolutism' under the cloak of progressive and oppositional thought and practice. He writes:

> "Striving to be both European and black requires some specific forms of double consciousness. By saying this I do not mean to suggest that taking on either or both of these unfinished

identities necessarily exhausts the subjective resources of any particular individual. However, where racist, nationalist, or ethnically absolutist discourses orchestrate political relationships so that these identities appear to be mutually exclusive, occupying the space between them or trying to demonstrate their continuity has been viewed as a provocative and even oppositional act of political insubordination." (1993, p.1)

It is the idea of identity as ever capable of being 'finished' against which Gilroy wishes to argue, and it is one of the characteristics of 'identity politics' that it has to implicitly or explicitly posit social and individual identity as an *essence*. The seemingly inescapable polarities of essentialist and pluralist ways of thinking dog the politics of race as they have dogged much social scientific and critical work. Integration and anti-racism must surely be understood as processes rather than events, in which a dialectic of *change* must be assumed if they are to mean what they claim to mean. Thus, we can imagine that the women (black and white) of Mantes-la-Jolie may, even if in small ways, come to experience themselves with altered identities as a consequence of new forms of interaction between them in the wake of the mayor's interventions. As Gilroy says of 'black England':

"Previously separated political and intellectual traditions converged, and in their coming together, overdetermined the process of black Britain's social and historical formation. This blending is misunderstood if it is conceived in simple ethnic terms, but right and left, racist and anti-racist, black and white tacitly share a view of it as little more than a collision between fully formed and mutually exclusive cultural communities." (1993, p.7)

From this conceptual ground, Gilroy has lent his weight to work which re-evaluates an unquestioning commitment to 'same race placement' policies (Aldridge and Gaber 1994). Buried in current discourses about racial identity which inform child protection and child care practices there is, arguably, a 'myth of origins' in which the restoration of the abandoned child can only be achieved by the construction of a positive identity conceived in terms of cultural 'roots'. Within French political discourse, the subsumption, but not the annihilation, of notions of identity within those of 'sociality', the recognition that all personal identities are social, multifarious and changing, may offer something worthwhile in the effort to reconstruct a social work politics which reconciles attention to 'differences' within a universalised struggle to create 'the good society'.

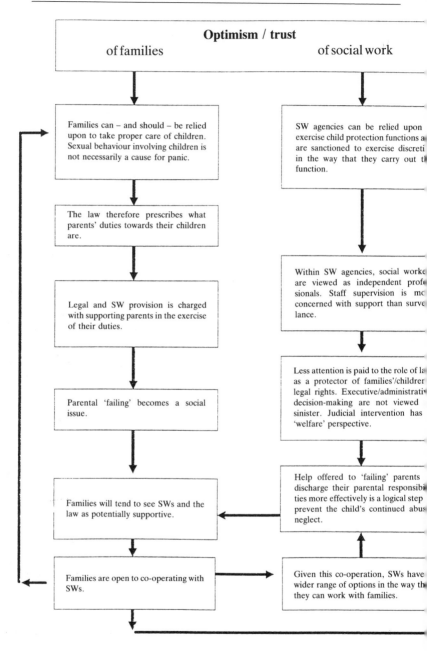

Figure 4

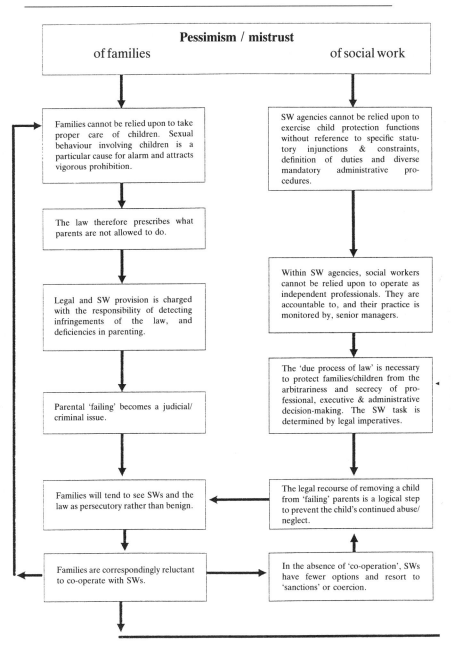

Figure 5

Cycles of hope and counsels of despair

We suspect that in subtle but important ways, the universalist
tendencies of French political thought contribute to the professional culture of 'optimism' noted in the last chapter, and which
is an observable feature of the day to day practice of child
protection workers, in marked contrast to that of England. The
progress of one French case observed by an English worker
involved a single mother, her cohabitee, and her 15-year-old
daughter living in the same household. The daughter had been
truanting from school, using drugs and, it was believed, having
unprotected sex with her boyfriend. The mother had approached
the Children's Judge directly 'in despair'. No legal order was in
force, but a period of 'observation and assessment' had been
recommended by the judge, and a combination of family and
individual work with the young woman set in train by the
éducatrice. The English practitioner expressed surprise that his
French counterpart did not consider the girl's *under age* sexual
activity to be a matter of concern. "Is this not a child protection
matter in France?" he mused. "Were it in England I would want to
know the circumstances, I would be concerned, because she is
having sex before the age of consent." Instead the social worker
was focusing on family relationships, and communication between
mother and daughter, as well as the mother's depression. Once
again, Lisa Appignanasi is succinct in identifying culturally
different attitudes to sexuality in France:

> "This is not the country of the shuddering liberal conscience or
> sensitive puritan guilts. Policing here, it seems, is left to the
> police – and neither internalised, nor taken on board by self-
> designated representatives of the greater good.
>
> "Nowhere is this clearer than in the sexual domain. What on
> American campuses would risk instant charges of ocular
> harrassment is a thoroughly acceptable and minute by minute
> occurrence. Step out into the street or into the metro and male
> eyes in any colour face assess you – tickle, tease, challenge,
> undress and pass on to the next woman. No one seems to
> mind...Nor is the traffic one way. Visiting men friends confide
> that they love the brazenness of women's eyes on them...
>
> "What has grown clear to me over my months here is that
> whereas in the American and to a somewhat lesser extent
> British imagination, sex is now coupled with fear of violence,
> this is not the case in France. It is not that there is no sexual
> violence here, no rape or child abuse ... But the instant
> and immediate equation of sex and violence is not made."
> (1994).

As with 'race relations', and notwithstanding the much more widespread and organised presence of a racist right wing in French politics, Appignanasi is speaking of the comparative lack of anxiety about these matters in day to day 'social intercourse'. There is no shortage of questioning feminist thought in France – this is the nation which has given us Simone de Beauvoir, Julia Kristeva and Hélène Cixous. But significantly, the latter two women have achieved prominence within feminist thought for their attempt to carve out a positive conceptual space for feminine identity and thus escape the strictures of being 'for or against' men, inside or outside the patriarchy.

With a whole range of concerns which have been drawn into the ambit of child protection practice in England, it appears that in France there is a prevailing attitude that given time, good professional help, the presence of a benign authority, and a determination to interfere only when absolutely necessary, people may be able to handle matters for themselves. If the apparent cohesion of French society in terms of shared norms and values, or at least shared debates about these, has its claustrophobic side, equally it has its liberating aspect too. Figure 4. illustrates how a cycle of trust and optimism in social work-family relationships can be seen to operate in a positively reinforcing manner. As we have suggested, 'trust' in this context is both individual and attitudinal, but also social and ideological. Figure 5. shows how pessimism and mistrust may operate in a similar cycle of reinforcement and reproduction.

As we have seen, the Hobbesian vision of a hypothetical state of nature in which the life of man is "nasty, brutish and short", and only the sovereign and the law stand between us and the war of all against all, prefigures both our adversarial system of justice and our political pluralism. As we noted in chapter 8, the ideals of the French Revolution include fraternity, the bond *between* people, as one of the preconditions of hope and freedom, and it is not unreasonable to see here the abstract foundations of the inter-dependency which in the French *conscience collective* marks relationships between Children's Judges and families, families and social workers, women and men, black people and white people.

Section Four
French Lessons

Chapter 11: Making the Children Act Work

Social work and the law: reconciling social reality and social expectations

The role of law is to organise social expectations. It strives to render the world predictable, manageable and therefore amenable to hard and fast judgements. The traditional role of social work, by contrast, has been to respond to unpredictable, messy and invariably complex, human situations. The law generates certainty but the stock in trade of social work is uncertainty.

When confronted with a mother who neglects or beats her young child a judge may say that she must stop this behaviour, assume her parental responsibilities and offer the kind of care that we might reasonably expect from a parent.

The social worker may say that as an emotionally deprived person, the mother may herself need to experience a consistent, caring relationship if she is to mature sufficiently to respond to the emotional needs of her child.

Both may be true and so a response which reconciles the social expectations expressed through the law and the social reality of a deeply embedded emotional problem articulated in the social work assessment is required. This is, of course, a familiar story in both France and England and this book has been concerned with the ways in which the claims of law and the claims of social work are reconciled in the two countries.

It is our view that because of the peculiar relationship between social work and the law established in England and Wales during the 1980s, but rooted in an ideology of the 1680s, such a reconciliation has become far more difficult to achieve. Viewed from England, the meeting in cabinet between the French Children's Judge, the social worker and the family appears to offer a space for the dialogue between social expectations and social reality which has been drastically eroded in the child protection

146

system of England and Wales in the past decade.

A core task, perhaps the core task, of a child protection system is to provide a space in which these two discourses, one concerning the establishment or reaffirmation of social expectations, rights and responsibilities and the other concerning responses to, and the management of, a complex and sometimes chaotic social reality, can become a single dialogue. A place where the competing claims of justice and welfare, of rules and needs, of guilt and suffering can take place. Perhaps one of the measures of an effective and fair system is that it provides sufficient, we could say optimal, space and time for this dialogue to occur.

The legal monologue

As we have argued, in England and Wales in the recent period social work and its discourse has been annexed by the law. Its concepts and theories have been simplified, proceduralised and transformed into 'theory-evidence'. Its professional authority has been supplanted by its statutory duties. Professional assessments have been displaced by evidential checklists and social workers' inter-personal skills have been prest into the service of evidence gathering.

This is no dialogue between social expectations and social reality but rather, as Michael King (1991) has argued, an annexation by the law, in which the social work role has been transformed into, and subordinated to, the imperatives of due process. Questions of 'evidence' and 'proof' have displaced considerations of 'need' and 'suffering'.

Yet, somewhat paradoxically, even as their professional authority was being eroded, the power shifts and redesignation of roles occasioned by the legal and managerial annexation of professional social work effectively handed social workers the responsibility for investigating and 'prosecuting' child protection cases.

At the same time, however, the Act enjoined social workers to work in 'partnership' with the multiplicity of family members and 'significant others' to whom the Act had offered an opportunity to become legal protagonists in the proceedings. Understandably, such a 'partnership' between people who are required to enter the legal arena as 'adversaries', has proved to be largely untenable. The Act aimed to create the basis for partnership yet, because legal and managerial annexation had transformed the social worker into a legal protagonist, indeed an agent of the law, engaged in an adversarial conflict with the families, and sometimes the children as well, this objective was subverted.

This raises the question of why the English system manages to effect so many more permanent separations of children and families than the French system, in which all those legally inadmissible social work concerns which, according to the dominant legal viewpoint jeopardise the interests of families, remain in play. Beyond this, it seems fairly evident that the French system, by dint of its flexibility, the absence of due process, the complementary roles played by judges and social workers which permits a dialogue between their two discourses, and its institutionalised optimism, promotes and fosters the very partnership which continues to elude our own system.

As we have noted, in the period when the child protection system of England and Wales was being annexed by the law, we saw the creation of the 'case conference', an entity which attempted to operate a more flexible 'shadow' system in which the discourse of social reality could be articulated. It was attended by representatives of the police and all relevant health and social welfare agencies, and had the power to decide whether to place a child on the local 'at risk' or 'child protection' register.

Initially it occupied a space between social work and the law, diverting some cases away from the legal process towards social agencies and monitoring developments in others in order to respond to changes in levels of help and support required. Latterly, it too has been subject to legal and managerial annexation and has come increasingly to resemble a quasi-judicial dress rehearsal for impending court appearances.

So it was that at the beginning of the 1990s British social workers found themselves in a system in which they had limited power, increased responsibility, enjoined to work in partnership with people whom the law had located in an adversarial relationship with them. It was a position which flowed logically from the institutionalised animosity to which we have referred in previous chapters. The mismatch between the power they held and the responsibilities they carried meant that they were destined to lead lives of high anxiety in which the attractions of a conservative practice, geared to the demands of self preservation rather than the needs of children and families, would be hard to resist.

Where do we go from here?

In previous chapters we have discussed the struggle between welfare and justice which took place in British child care from the mid-1970s. The 1989 Children Act, in the spirit of the Short Report, attempted to achieve a synthesis or reconciliation of the two. However, because it attempted to do this in a period when the cultural, ideological and political climate was profoundly hostile to the claims of 'welfare', the Act has been unable to fulfil its true potential.

The Act, like the Short Report before it, held out the promise of a new and potentially creative role for the law in enabling the family to resolve its own difficulties. This was an integrated child protection system in which the twin discourses of law and social reality became a problem-solving dialogue.

Had the Act been allowed to operate in the way that its architects intended, we would now be in a far better position to learn from the French experience than we are. For it is not, as is sometimes argued, the law which places a stumbling block in the path of the development of more effective child protection social work. In fact, it is a particularly narrow and restrictive inter-pretation of the law and the administrative constraints to which that interpretation have given rise which pose the problem. This legal/managerialist domination of child protection social work has also served to obscure the fact that vital resources and services for the families with whom social workers work are being steadily eroded.

But if the British child protection system was able to learn lessons from this other system, what would they be?

Resources

As we noted in Chapter 2, services for families are better resourced in France. Family allowances are higher and, because there are more health visitors than in Britain, children up to the age of six are visited by them regularly, and if they are at risk, frequently. Nursery school places are available for virtually all children of three-year-old and above and so the 'safety net' of care, prevention and surveillance has far fewer, and much smaller, holes in it than in Britain. Despite a current shortage of generic social workers in France, the clients of French social workers will usually see them more frequently and over a longer period, if they need to. For their part, the social workers have access to a wider range of specialist workers who can offer advice and supervision as well as undertake particular aspects of an intervention. An important resource available to social workers is the *Inspecteur* who carries power and responsibility for child protection cases before they enter the legal arena, and the Children's Judge who assumes this responsibility following such a referral. We identify these two figures as a resource since their existence serves to assuage the potentially immobilising anxieties which child-protection social work generates, and thus contributes to the efficiency and the effectiveness of workers.

Social workers and the law

It is not difficult for a French worker to refer a case to the Children's Judge. Such a referral does not require lengthy reports and is determined by the social worker's perception of the level of risk, the preparedness of the parents to co-operate with the social worker and, ultimately, the social worker's assessment of the child's suffering. As a result, French social workers do not find themselves in the position of having great anxieties about a child's safety and unco-operative parents, but no legally admissible evidence with which to transform their concerns into action. Although French social workers may not always agree with the judge, the fact that their authority is seen to stem from the judge gives them greater confidence in their own authority as they discharge their day to day responsibilities. Unlike some of their English counterparts, French social workers do not feel that it is they who are being judged.

Intervention takes place earlier, not least because of the availability of resources with which to undertake such intervention, and this means that social workers have more opportunity to work with the family while change is still possible.

When it is working well, and of course this is neither always nor everywhere, the French child protection system achieves the kind of dialogue between social reality and social expectations which enables effective intervention with families in cases of neglect and abuse. This dialogue is facilitated by a better distribution of space, power, authority and responsibility, between children, their parents, social workers and judges than has thus far been achieved in the English system.

Space

Each of the protagonists in French child protection proceedings is afforded access to the judge, a space in which they can say what they need to say in a 'language' which does justice to what they think, feel and believe.

They are also given a shared space, the *audience*, presided over by the judge who is fluent in the language of social reality and social need, the language of law and social expectations, the vernacular language of angry or dispirited parents and the sometimes non-verbal or inarticulate language of damaged and abused children and young people. This fluency is a product of their close association and joint work with professionals in the policing, health and child welfare fields. As a result, the judge often commands sufficient trust to act as an interpreter of language and meaning, a promotor of dialogue between the other protagonists. Importantly, none of these languages, or discourses, needs to be transformed into something it is not in order to be included in the dialogue.

The judge carries sufficient formal authority to decide who should occupy this shared space at any given time, including the witnesses they choose to call, and such decisions are made on the basis of an assessment by the judge of the vulnerabilities of the protagonists involved in the proceedings. Only rarely would a professional legal representative speak on behalf of any of the protagonists because this would discourage the dialogue, the development of which is the primary function of the *audience*.

Power

The possibility of a dialogue between the protagonists at the *audience* is inextricably linked with the power of the judge to effect a permanent separation between parents and children. Power and authority are not synonymous and an interesting feature of French child protection proceedings, in which Children's Judges do not have the power to effect such a permanent separation, is that decisions which mean that a child will effectively live away from their family for a protracted period, if not permanently, are usually reached by a process of negotiation. Beyond this, because less is at stake, and the consequences of involvement in child protection proceedings are not perceived as irrevocable, protagonists will normally enter the proceedings on the basis of less 'evidence' and at an earlier point. When they do so, they tend to be in a more relaxed and less hostile frame of mind than is often the case in England and Wales. It appears that, contrary to the popular Anglo-Saxon view, this relative lack of power enhances the authority of the judge.

Authority and responsibility

In France, the judge and the social worker work as a team with the former commissioning and monitoring the intervention and the latter executing it. This appears to distribute authority and responsibility in a way which reduces the anxieties of all parties.

Child protection proceedings in England and Wales take the form of several days of serial monologue, often transmogrified into a barely comprehensible legal discourse by a highly paid legal professional. In France they take the form of a, frequently protracted, dialogue between the protagonists which reflects an optimistic belief in the possibility of change.

If the objective of the 1989 Act was, in part, to divert more child protection cases from the courts through the 'minimum intervention principle' and the legitimation of a partnership philosophy, the organisation and, more importantly, the valorisation of the 'administrative sphere' must hold the key. In France the figure of the *Inspecteur* appears to be the non-judicial embodiment of the social contract between citizens, professionals and the 'state'. The *Inspecteur* carries authority, exercises power, and implements welfare strategies in the context of a consensus about 'good enough child care'. We cannot borrow this consensus from France, but we can, and in view of the authors of this book, should, turn our attention to how such a civil consensus might be encouraged and supported by organisational reform of the administrative sphere in child protection work.

Systems and communication

In both the English and French child protection systems, information exchange between professionals and systems is crucially important. In France the main forum for co-operation and communication is the multi-disciplinary team of the CISS (area office), and assessment and case management is shared within the agency. In England this forum is the case conference and assessment and case management is shared between the agencies. While there were concerns about inter-agency communication in both countries this was far more muted in France. It is possible that, with fewer professionals involved, the regular team meetings of CISS provide a more effective means of channelling information than the English case conference.

Communication between professionals is affected by the legal system in which they work. The modern case conference reflects the adversarial system of the English courts and the meetings of CISS reflect the inquisitorial nature of the French courts. An adversarial system invites people to come and present their monologue. An inquisitorial system asks people to participate in a dialogue. Inquisitorial systems actively seek understanding. Adversarial systems are reactive, seeking evidence to substantiate assertions. Thus, it may well be that the structure and culture of the English case conference is impeding its intended function; to give a fair hearing to parents and facilitate the flow of information between professionals.

Prevention and supervision

One striking feature of the French system was the effectiveness of supervision orders which, in half of the cases we studied, were extended at the request of the families. In France judicial and administrative supervision orders are used extensively. In England supervision orders are used only infrequently, despite the fact that they have been strengthened by the 1989 Act.

Because the French system is inquisitorial and 'welfare-oriented', a 'whole-case', holistic, approach can be adopted by the social worker. The location of the authority for the intervention in an individual, an *Inspecteur* or a judge appears to facilitate the development of trust between the social worker and the family and as such, creates a sound basis for a preventative partnership. By contrast, the English system, being rights-based and adversarial, is geared to the legitimation of the rights of one party to the proceedings over those of the others. This tends to be inimical to the type of preventive partnership which is an obvious feature of social work undertaken under the auspices of a supervision order in France.

Adoption and permanency

There is a striking difference between French and English attitudes to adoption. Through comparison we became aware of the ways in which the possibility of adoption as a 'solution' came to influence the final outcome in the English cases we studied. It appeared to the French social workers that the possibility of adoption in the English system discourages the search for alternative solutions. This led us to reconsider what English social workers mean by 'drift'. Some situations described by English social workers as being in 'drift' were perceived by French social workers, as 'stable'. It appears that, in England, as a result of the availability of the adoption solution, we are far more prepared to move children around between a number of short term placements in order to eventually achieve a permanent placement. We are prepared to sacrifice short term stability for eventual permanence. French workers, by contrast, were concerned to achieve stability in the short or medium term as a base from which to undertake the long term task of rehabilitation with the natural family.

Conclusion

France is not paradise and the message from this book is not that we should import French practices lock, stock and barrel. Comparative research of the type we have described here reveals important differences between child protection systems, differences from which we can learn, but it also causes us to look at our own systems and practices differently. It makes us question the taken-for-granted world we usually inhabit and asks us to disinter our values and assumptions and scrutinise them afresh.

It is our hope that, in presenting our experiences to the reader, we have been able to convey something of this process and that this may have triggered a similar response in them. If it has, this book has succeeded.

Glossary of French Terms

Judicial and Social Work Measures

Adoption simple: The broad equivalent of 'open adoption' in England, but much more rarely used.

AEMO (Action Éducative en Milieu Ouvert) Judiciare: A judicial order on a child or children imposed by the Children's Judge usually for a period of one or two years, while the child remains at home. A judicial AEMO is broadly comparable to a supervision order in the English system.

AEMO administrative: A non-judicial order authorised by ASE, the specialist child care service of the local authority. It creates a contract for the use of resources between the family and the social worker.

Assistance éducative: The general term for social work intervention with children and families, whether in an administrative or a judicial framework.

Assistance éducative dans le cadre d'une mesure de placement: The imposition by the Children's Judge of a placement to provide *assistance éducative*. This could be in a residential home, with foster parents or with a trusted third party. Such a measure could be short term *(ordonnance)* or long term *(jugement)*.

Audience: A hearing with a family in the office *(cabinet)* of the Children's Judge. The atmosphere and setting of the hearing is informal, presided over by the judge, but without ceremony or robes. The family's social worker will usually be present, but rarely any lawyers.

Conditions d'éducation gravement compromisés: 'Conditions of upbringing which are severely compromised' – the criteria which informs a decision to refer a child protection case to the Children's

Judge. The condition does not have to be proved and the law of 1989 relating to the protection of children states that where a child is 'a victim of ill-treatment, or is presumed to be so, and it is impossible to assess the situation, or the family manifestly refuse to accept the intervention of the ASE', the case should be referred to the judicial authority without delay.

Hebergement: A system of foster care, often with a relative, where a child stays with its natural parents for a night or more on a regular basis.

Jugement sur le fond: A longer term renewable decision (up to a maximum of two years) made by a judge with respect to a child. A judicial AEMO of more than six months would be of this kind, and often referred to simply as a *jugement.*

Mesure: A court order enforced by the Children's Judge.

Mesure de Liberté Surveillée: A probation order for Juveniles.

Mesure de tutelle des prestations d'allocation familiale: An order made by the Children's Judge allowing supervision of a family's finances and budgeting.

OMO (Observation en Milieau Ouvert): An assessment order, similar to an Interim Supervision Order.

Ordonnance: A short term and provisional (six months) statutory order made by a Children's Judge with respect to a child.

Revenu Minimum d'Insertion (RMI): A guaranteed minimum benefit introduced by the government in 1988 for those who agree to undertake education, training or voluntary work. The scheme aims at 'reinsertion' into society of people marginalised by unemployment, homelessness or other factors, and social workers have a central role in its implementation.

Saisin: An order requiring a case to come before a judge.

Commonly Used Terms

Éducation: One of the central concepts of French social work, it denotes something much broader than just teaching or learning, including the idea of the child's total social, emotional, and environmental development and well-being.

Exclusion: *Exclusion* and its counterpart *inclusion* are difficult concepts to define accurately, and the subject of continuing debate in France. 'Marginalisation' is a close translation, implying structural exclusion from basic resources, opportunities and social processes. Unemployment, homelessness, and ill health are often cited as the three core dimensions of *exclusion*, but many other groupings such as prisoners, the disabled, and psychiatric patients may be associated with the idea of *les exclus*.

Inclusion: *Inclusion* carries strong connotations of social 'belonging' through structural access to resources and opportunities, and hence to full participation in society and citizenship.

Insertion social: Closely related to *inclusion* and *intégration* 'social insertion' is concerned with a systematic attack on poverty, social marginalisation, youth crime and other forms of *exclusion*. The central plank of *insertion* as social policy was the introduction in 1988 of the *Revenu Minimum d'Insertion (RMI)*, a guaranteed minimum benefit in exchange for which '*RMIstes*' contract into training, education or employment schemes. The idea of *insertion is often broadened to include what we in England would call 'prevention' or community work.*

Intégration: Sometimes used as a synonym for *insertion*, the term more often refers to an ideology of racial integration. 'Immigrants', many of whom until recently had automatic rights to French citizenship, have been the object of 'integrationist' policy. Some of the founding principles of the French Republic such as 'secularity' would be in tension with policies promoting the cultural or religious specificity of immigrant communities, although in the last decade there has been a greater emphasis on integration which respects difference rather than promoting assimilation.

Pedagogie: The theory and practice of guiding the process of children and young people's growth, development and socialisation. Closely related to *éducation* as a basic principle informing social work in France.

Placement: A placement for a child.

Prévention: Concerns the legal requirement on local authorities to establish projects in disadvantaged areas which work against social marginalisation. These interventions are closer to what we think of as 'community work' or 'community development' in Britain, and are related to the wider project of *insertion*.

Social Services Personnel

Assistante maternelle: A foster parent or childminder who cares for children on a daytime basis.

Assistante social de secteur: A local authority social worker who will normally be a 'generalist' with responsibility for a small 'sector' of the population – or patch.

Commission d'Évaluation: A meeting of the CISS multi-disciplinary team to review cases. This is the first point of consultation for the *assistante social de secteur*. The commission makes a collective response and advises the *assistante social*.

Commission de Placement: A meeting of the CISS multi-disciplinary team to discuss recommendations for a child's placement. Relevant workers from other statutory and voluntary agencies may be invited to attend.

Commission de Prévention: A meeting of the CISS multi-disciplinary team attended by the *Inspecteur* who must gain parental consent for the course of action proposed by the commission, unless it proposes referral to the Children's Judge.

Éducateur spécialisé: A social worker trained in the principle of *éducation* to work with children, young people and their families.

Éducateur de jeunes enfants: A social worker trained in the practice of *éducation* to work with young children, usually in day care or residential settings.

Famille d'accueil: A foster family.

Inspecteur: The central figure in the 'administrative' sphere of French child protection. Not necessarily social work trained, she or he is responsible for formal assessment processes with respect to families with children at risk, for deciding on the implementation of *AEMO administratives*, and for making referrals to the Children's Judge.

Psychologue: A psychologist. They are much more widely employed in front line social work services than in Britain.

Travailleur social: The generic term for all varieties of French social worker.

Travailleuse familiale: Equivalent to a family aid in Britain.

Tutrice/Tutelle: A social worker attached to either the DISS or the CNAF (see this glossary) whose role is to help with family budgeting.

Judicial Services and Personnel

COAE – Consultation d'Orientation et d'Action Éducative: A service of the DPJJ which works closely with the Children's Judge.

A multi-disciplinary team which carries out observation orders and assessments in the community. The team will give an expert opinion to the judge before a long term decision or order is made.

DPJJ – Direction de la Protection Judiciare et de la Jeunesse: This is a state service with a local organisation in each *Département*. Established in 1945 to work with juvenile delinquents, this is still its major role, but services like COAE are extensively involved in child protection assessment and short term work.

Gendarmerie: The regional police force who would be involved in child protection cases on the rare occasions when police are called in.

Juge pour Enfants: Sometimes called the *juge d'enfants* or the *juge des enfants*, she or he is the central figure in the judicial sphere of the French child protection system. A *magistrat de jugement*, the judge is responsible for all cases involving juvenile delinquency or children at risk, and undertakes the same three year advanced training course as all other judges. The judge has a wide range of powers with respect to children who come before the court, but not the power to separate a child from its parents permanently.

Magistrat de Jugement: Also called magistrates of the bench, they are independent of any political authority, and their role is to judge. The *juge des enfants* is a *magistrat de jugement*.

Police: The police have a limited role in child protection work in France and can only be called in on the order of a judge. In many cases where prosecution of an abuser is seen as appropriate, civil application by the parents or relatives will be encouraged.

SEAT – Service Éducatif Auprès du Tribunal: Each High Court *(Tribunal de Grande Instance)* has a SEAT service attached to undertake emergency investigations on the authority of the judge.

Tribunal de Grande Instance: The High Court with responsibilities including the jurisdiction of minors.

Tribunal d'Instance: The lower court, comparable to an English magistrates court, but staffed by trained judges, as are all French courts.

Parquet: The *Parquet* is an office of the High Court administered by the Home Office. The *Parquet* can take the initiative in bringing proceedings or become a party during proceedings to represent the interests of the state. Apart from *Magistrats de Jugement* the magistrates of the *Parquet* are the other main group of magistrates working in the High Court.

Procureur: The deputy magistrate of the *Parquet* responsible for minors who receives all child abuse referrals from social services, the police or the citizen.

Other Organisations and Services

ASE – Aide Sociale à l'Enfance: The specialist children's social service within all local authorities, ASE is at the centre of the system of administrative protection for children.

Associations: A general term for 'voluntary organisations' which are very widespread in France and much more influential than in England.

Caisse Allocation Familiale: The arm of the social security service responsible for family benefits.

Centre Medico Psycho-Pedagogic: A service for children with emotional or behavioural problems similar to a child and family guidance clinic.

CNAF – Caisse Nationale d'Allocation Familiales: The organisation within the French social security system responsible for distributing family allowances.

CISS – Circonscription d'Intervention Sanitaires et Sociales: A district of the local authority social services (DISS). Each départment (county) is divided into a number of geographical areas *(Circonscriptions)* of about 50,000 inhabitants, each of which is covered by a multi-disciplinary team. Each *Circonscription* is divided into sectors covered by one *assistante social*. Thus a local authority generic social worker is often known as an *assistante social de secteur*. The system has some resemblence to 'patch' organisation in Britain.

Conseil General: The elected local authority.

DISS/DASS – Direction d'Interventions Sanitaires et Sociales: The social services department of the local authority.

EMP (Externa Medico-Psychiatric): A day hospital for children with medical, psychiatric or behavioural problems.

Équipe de prévention: 'Prevention teams' set up under President Mitterand's drive against *exclusion* in the early 1980s. All local authorities are required by statute to have preventative services in disadvantaged areas. Their approach has more in common with 'community work' or 'social action' than 'preventative casework'.

Foyer de l'enfance/Maison d'enfants: A children's home.

IME (Institut Medico Educative): A residential establishment for children with medical, psychiatric or behavioural problems.

Maison d'enfants à caractère sociale: A centre for the reception and treatment of children put in the care of ASE by their parents or under order.

Pouponnière: A residential nursery which is seen to offer supplementary rather than alternative attachments to the natural family.

PMI – Protection Maternelle et Infantile: The public health service, available to all, for mothers-to-be and for parents with children up to the age of six. They work preventatively but with special responsibility for situations where a child is at risk. PMI employs a range of medical and paramedical staff including specialist community nurses for children, similar to English health visitors.

PMI (Protection Maternelle & Infantile): A universal public health service for mothers, and children under six years of age. PMI also undertakes preventive work with families where there are difficulties, or the children are perceived to be in danger.

Secteur Associatif: The 'voluntary sector'.

Bibliography

Aldridge, J. and Gabor, I. (1994) *In the Best Interests of the Child*, London, Free Association Books

Aldridge, M. (1990) 'Social Work and the News Media: A Hopeless Case?', in *Br. J. Social Wk*, 20, pp.611-625

Appignanasi, L. (1994) 'Liberté, Égalité and Fraternité: PC and the French', in Dunnant, S. (ed), *The War of the Words*, London, Virago, pp.145-63

Ashford, D. (1988) *The Emergence of the Welfare State*, London, Blackwell

Ball, C., Harris, R., Roberts, G. & Vernon, S. (1988) *The Law Report*, London, CCETSW

Baudouin, J-M. (1990) *Le Juge des Enfants*, Paris, ESF

Baker, J. (1986) 'Comparing national priorities: family and population policies in Britain and France', in *Journal of Social Policy*, 15 (4), pp.421-41

Baldock (1989) 'United Kingdom – A Perpetual Crisis in Marginality', in Munday B. (ed) *The Crisis in Welfare: an International Perspective on Social Services and Social Work*, Harvester Wheatsheaf

Barre, S. (1993) *Le Placement de l'Enfant en France et en Angleterre: le Role du Travailleur Social*, Paris, Fondation pour l'Enfance

Bonnemaison (1982) *Juvenile Delinquency; Suppression and Solidarity*, Paris

Bullock, R. (1993) The United Kingdom, in Colton, M. J. and Hellinckx, W. *Child Care in the EC*, Cambridge, Cambridge University Press

Bullock, R., Little, M. and Millham, S. (1993) *Going Home*, Aldershot, Dartmouth

Cannan, C., Berry, L. and Lyons, K. (1992) *Social Work and Europe*, London, Macmillan

Cannan, C. (1993), *Changing Families, Changing Welfare: Family Centres and the Welfare State* London, Harvester Wheatsheaf

CEC (1990) *Child Care in Europe 1985-1990*, European Commission, Brussels

CEC (1993) *European Community Childcare Network Annual Report for 1992*, European Commission, Brussels

Chamberlyne, P. (1991), 'New Directions in Welfare? France, West Germany, Italy and Britain in the 1980s', in *Critical Social Policy*, 33 pp.5-39

Chauvière, M. (1980) *Enfance Inadaptée: L'héritage d'Vichy Paris*, Edition Ouvrières

Chester, R. (1994) 'Flying without Instruments or Flight Plans: Family Policy in the United Kingdom' in Commission of European Communities DGV, European Observatory on National Family Policies, Brussells, The European Commission

Clarke, J. Cochrane, A. and McLaughlin, E. (1994) *Managing Social Policy*, London, Sage

Cochrane and Clarke (1993) *Comparing Welfare States – Britain in International Context*, London, Sage

Cohen, B. (1993), 'Childcare Policy in the European Community: finding a place for children', in Simpson, R. and Walker, R. (1993) *Europe: for Richer or Poorer?*, CPAG, Blackmore

Colambani, C. (1982) 'Les "Lieux de vie" et l'affaire du Coral I. Une campagne et une enquete', in *Le Monde*, 28th November, 1982, p.9, par.3

Colton, M. J. and Hellinckx, W. (1993) *Child Care in the EC*, Cambridge, Cambridge University Press

Commaille, J. (1994), 'France: from a Family Policy to Policies towards the Family', in Dumon, W. (ed), *Changing Family Policies in the Member States of the European Union*

Cooper, A. (1987), 'Neighbourhood and Network: A Model from Practice', in Darvill, G. and Smale, G. (eds), *Partners in Empowerment*, London, NISW

Cooper, A. (1992a), 'Anxiety and Child Protection Work in Two National Systems', in *Journal of Social Work Practice*, 6 (2), pp.117-28

Cooper, A. (1992b) *Methodological and Epistemological Considerations in Cross-National Comparative Research*, London, CCSWS

Cooper, A., Freund, V., Grevot, A., Hetherington, R. and Pitts, J. (1992) *The Social Work Role in Child Protection: An Anglo-French Comparison*, London, CCSWS

Cooper, A. (1994), 'In Care or en Famille? Child Protection, the Family and the State in France and England', in *Social Work in Europe*, 1 (1)

Corbillon, M. (1993), France, in Colton, M. J. and Hellinckx, W. *Child Care in the EC*, Cambridge, Cambridge University Press

Davies, M. & Sale, A. (1989) *Child Protection in Europe*, London NSPCC

Dennington, J. and Pitts, J. (1991) *Developing Services for Young People in Crisis*, London, Longman

DHSS (1985) *Review of Child Care Law: Report to Ministers of an Inter-Departmental Working Party*, London, HMSO

Dyson, K. (1980) *The State Tradition in Western Europe*, Oxford, Martin Robertson

Ely, P. and Stanley, C. (1990) *The French Alternative: Delinquency, Prevention and Child Protection in France*, London, NACRO

Eurodata (1991) (Reported in *The Guardian*, Boseley, S. 'European Poll finds faith in UK schools has faded'), 12/2/91

Eurostats (1994) *Households and Families in the European Union*, Rapid Reports: Population and Social Conditions

Ferri, E. and Saunders, A. (1991) *Parents, Professionals and Pre-School Centres: A Study of Barnado's Provision*, London, National Children's Bureau

Fisher, M. (1986) *In and Out of Care*, London, Batsford

Fletcher, B. [1993] *Not Just a Name* London, Who Cares Trust & The National Consumer Council

Foucault, M. (1986) 'What is Enlightenment?' in Rabinow, P. [ed] *The Foucault Reader*, Harmondsworth, Peregrine

Fourniér, J., Questiaux, N. and Delarue, J-M. (1989) *Traite du Social Situation Luttes, Politiques, Institutions*, 5th Edition, Paris, Dalioz

Fox Harding, L. (1991) *Perspectives in Child Care Policy*, London, Longman

Freeman, M. (1992) *Children, their Families and the Law*, London, Macmillan

Gilroy, P. (1993) *The Black Atlantic*, London, Verso

Girodet, D. (1990) 'France', in Sale, A. and Davies, M. (eds) *Child Protection Policies and Practice in Europe*, London, NSPCC

Greenland, C. (1987) *Preventing CAN Deaths: An International Study of Deaths Due to Child Abuse and Neglect*, London, Tavistock Publications

Grevot, A. (1994) 'The Child Protection System of England and Wales seen through French Eyes', *Social Work in Europe*, 1 (1), pp.39-41

Habermas, J. (1971) *Towards a Rational Society* London, Heinemann Educational

Hadjisky, E. (1987) On First Contact With Abuse and Neglect *Journal of Social Work Practice* 3. pp.31-7

Hall, S., Critcher, C., Jefferson, T., Clarke, J. and Roberts, B. (1978) *Policing the Crisis: Mugging, the State and Law and Order*, London, Macmillan

Hantrais, L., (1993), 'Towards a Europeanisation of Family Policy?', in Simpson, R. and Walker, R. (1993) *Europe: for Richer or Poorer?* London, CPAG, Blackmore

Hantrais, L. (1994) 'Comparing Family Policy in Britain, France and Germany', in *Journal of Social Policy*, 23, 2, pp.135-160

Hayek, F. (1944) *The Road to Serfdom*, London, Routledge

Hetherington, R., Cooper, A. and Grevot, A. (1993) *The French System of Child Protection*, London, CCSWS

Hetherington, R. (1994) 'Trans-Manche Partnerships', in *Adoption and Fostering*, 18 (3), pp.17-20

Hill, M. (ed) (1991) 'Social Work and the European Community, Research Highlights' in *Social Work* 23, London, Jessica Kingsley

HMSO (1991) *Working Together Under the Children Act 1989*, London

Hocquenhem, G. (1983) *Les Petits Garcons*, Paris, Allain Michel

Jeunesse Culture Loisirs Technique (JCLT), West London Institute, CNFEPJJ Ministère de la Justice (1994) *Le role du Travail Socio-Éducatif dans la Protection de l'Enfance, une Comparaison Entre l'Angleterre et la France*, Paris, Editions JCLT

Johanet, G. (1982) *La Nouvelle Politique Familiale* Paris, Droit Sociale

Kamerman, S. (1984) 'Women, Children and Poverty: Public Policies and Female-Headed Families in Industrialised Countries', in *Sigma*, 10 [2] pp.249-271

King, M. (1988) *Making Social Crime Prevention Work: The French Experience*, London, NACRO

King, M. (1991), 'Child Welfare in Law: the Emergence of a Hybrid Discourse in *Journal of Law and Society* 18 pp.218-236

King, M. and Piper, C. (1990) *How the Law Thinks about Children*, Aldershot, Gower

King, M. and Trowell, J. (1992), *Children's Welfare and the Law: The Limits of Legal Intervention*, London, Sage

London Borough of Brent (1985) *A Child In Trust, A Report of the Public Inquiry*

Lorenz, W. (1994) *Social Work in a Changing Europe*, London, Routledge

Menzies Lyth, I. (1960) 'A case study of the functioning of social systems as a defence against anxiety', in *Human Relations*, 13 (2)

Mills, C. W. (1959) *The Sociological Imagination*, Harmondsworth, Penguin

Moss, P. (1987) *A Review of Childminding Research*, London, Thomas Coram Research Unit

Munday, B. (1989) *The Crisis in Welfare: An International Perspective on Social Services and Social Work*, London, Harvester Wheatsheaf

Nava, M. (1988), 'Cleveland and the Press: Outrage and Anxiety in the Reporting of Child Sexual Abuse', in *Feminist Review*, 28, pp.103-121

Neubauer, E. (1992), Familienpolitische Ansätze zum Ausgliech der Aufwendungen für Kinder in *GEFAM Zwölf Wege der Familienpolitik in der Europäischen Gemeinschaft, Eigenständige Systeme und Vergleichbare Qualitäten?*, Vorläufiger Bericht zum Colloquium, Bonn, Chapter 7

Nixon, J. and Williamson, V. (1993) 'Returner and Retainer Policies for Women', in Jones, C. (ed) *New Perspectives on the Welfare State in Europe*, London, Routledge

Parton, N. (1985) *The Politics of Child Abuse*, London, Macmillan

Parton, N. (1991) *Governing the Family*, London, Macmillan

Peters, R. S. (1989), 'Hobbes' in Urmson J. O. & Ree, J. *The Concise Encyclopedia of Western Philosophy & Philosophers*, London, Unwin Hyman

Pitts, J. (1988) *The Politics of Juvenile Crime*, London, Sage

Pitts, J. (1990) *Working With Young Offenders*, London, BASW/Macmillan

Pitts, J. (1994), 'What Can We Learn in Europe?' in *Social Work in Europe*, 1 (1), pp.48-53

Popper, K. (1945) *The Open Society and its Enemies*, London, Routledge

Preston-Shoot, M. and Agass, D. (1990) *Making Sense of Social Work*, London, Macmillan

Regnault, P. (1994) Interview, in *Social Work in Europe*, 1 (1), June

Rorty, R. (1989) *Contingency, Irony and Solidarity*, Cambridge, Cambridge University Press

Rousseau, J. J. (1968) *The Social Contract and Discourses*, London, Dent

Schnapper, D. (1992) *L'Europe des Immigrés*, Paris, Editions François Bourin

Scott, A. (1988) Feminism and the Seductiveness of the "Real Event", *Feminist Reviews*, 28, pp.88-102

Simpson, R. & Walker, R. (1993) *Europe – For Richer or Poorer?*, London, CPAG

Social Services Committee (HC 360) (1984), *Children in Care*, London, HMSO (The Short Report)

Sorensen, A. (1989) 'Women's Economic Vulnerability: the Case of Single Mothers', a paper to EC conference on *Poverty, Marginalisation and Social Exclusion*, Alghero

Storr, D. (1994) Child Protection Conferences: Weighing Beliefs and Facts *Professional Social Work*, June p.6

Taylor, A. J. P. (1972) *An Introduction to the Communist Manifesto*, Harmondsworth, Penguin

Thévenet, A. (1990) *L'Aide Sociale Aujourd'hui*, Paris, ESF

Thorpe, D. et al (1980) *Out of Care*, George Allen & Unwin

Todd, E. (1991) *The Making of Modern France: Politics, Ideology and Culture*, London, Basil Blackwell

Veidier, P. (1988) 'Limited Adoption in France', in *Adoption and Fostering*, 12 (1)

Will, D. and Baird, D. (1984) 'An Integrated Approach to Professional Dysfunction in Systems', in *Journal of Family Therapy*, 6, pp.275-290

Woodhouse, D. and Pengelly, P. (1991) *Anxiety and the Dynamics of Collaboration*, Aberdeen, Aberdeen University Press

Wroe, A. (1988) *Social Work, Child Abuse and the Press*, Norwich, Social Work Monographs

Zizek, S. (1989) *The Sublime Object of Ideology*, London, Verso

Index

166